Marketing and Merchandising for Musicians

Robert Safir

Course Technology PTR
A part of Cengage Learning

COURSE TECHNOLOGY
CENGAGE Learning

Australia • Brazil • Japan • Korea • Mexico • Singapore • Spain • United Kingdom • United States

COURSE TECHNOLOGY
CENGAGE Learning®

Marketing and Merchandising for Musicians
Robert Safir

Publisher and General Manager, Course Technology PTR: Stacy L. Hiquet

Associate Director of Marketing: Sarah Panella

Manager of Editorial Services: Heather Talbot

Senior Marketing Manager: Mark Hughes

Acquisitions Editor: Orren Merton

Project Editor/Copy Editor: Cathleen D. Small

Interior Layout Tech: MPS Limited

Cover Designer: Luke Fletcher

Indexer: Larry Sweazy

Proofreader: Megan Belanger

For product information and technology assistance, contact us at
Cengage Learning Customer & Sales Support, 1-800-354-9706

For permission to use material from this text or product, submit all requests online at **www.cengage.com/permissions**

Further permissions questions can be emailed to
permissionrequest@cengage.com.

Starbucks and the Starbucks logo are registered trademarks of Starbucks. MySpace is a trademark of Myspace LLC. The NIKE name and the Swoosh design are owned, registered and/or licensed by NIKE. Apple and iTunes are registered trademarks of Apple Inc., registered in the U.S. and other countries. The Ford name is owned or used under license by Ford. Microsoft is a registered trademark of Microsoft Corporation in the United States and/or other countries. Best Buy and the Best Buy logo are trademarks or registered trademarks of BBY Solutions, Inc. Coca-Cola is a registered trademark of The Coca-Cola Company. McDonald's is a registered trademark owned by the McDonald's Corporation. Cisco is a registered trademark in the United States and certain other countries. Adobe is a registered trademark of Adobe Systems Incorporated in the United States and/or other countries. CafePress is a trademark in the United States and other countries. Google is a trademark of Google Inc. in the United States and other countries. Amazon Cloud Player is a trademark or trade dress of Amazon in the U.S. and other countries. All other trademarks are the property of their respective owners.

All images © Cengage Learning unless otherwise noted.

Library of Congress Control Number: 2011936047

ISBN-13: 978-1-4354-5800-0

ISBN-10: 1-4354-5800-1

Course Technology, a part of Cengage Learning
20 Channel Center Street
Boston, MA 02210
USA

Cengage Learning is a leading provider of customized learning solutions with office locations around the globe, including Singapore, the United Kingdom, Australia, Mexico, Brazil, and Japan. Locate your local office at: **international.cengage.com/region**

Cengage Learning products are represented in Canada by Nelson Education, Ltd.

For your lifelong learning solutions, visit **courseptr.com**

Visit our corporate website at **cengage.com**

Printed in the United States of America
1 2 3 4 5 6 7 14 13 12

I dedicate this book to all of the people in the creative arts, many of whom have seen their works either diminished in value or regarded as mere "content" in our evolving digital age. May the creative people in our world flourish today and in future generations, not only by having a means to survive and make a decent living, but also by being regarded as people whose talents and craftsmanship are cherished and highly valued by society.

As always, this book is dedicated to my family, whose constant encouragement and support make it possible to keep plugging away at goals that sometimes seem nebulous, intangible, or otherwise beyond my reach.

Finally, I dedicate this book to my parents, who never saw my published works but were key in pointing out the simple but important truths that guided me down the right path, creatively and otherwise.

Acknowledgments

I would like to thank the people at Cengage Learning, who always play an important role in imagining, producing, and delivering a book to market.

First, a thank you goes out to Orren Merton, the Coach of Coaches, who always says the right thing at the right time and never fails to keep the train rolling down the track. I don't know how he does it with so many books, so many times in a row.

Thank you to Cathleen Small, a dynamite editor whose contributions may be as small as a punctuation mark or as big as a "back-to-the-drawing-board" suggestion. She is a positive force who made me work harder and better.

Thank you to Megan Cooper, who helped me as a last-ditch effort to get images for the book without regard to hours that fell during evenings and weekends. She is another "can-do" type who rounded out the team that helped me complete this book.

Thank you to all of the industry experts who provided me with great interviews for Chapter 14, without regard to the usual "What do I get out of this?" They are busy people who went the extra yard to provide valuable information to the readers of this book, and I appreciate it very much.

And thank you to all the people in the music industry who said "You can" and to all the people in this business—and other people along the way—who said "You can't."

You might as well have said, "You can."

About the Author

Robert Safir is a Los Angeles–based composer, producer, recording engineer, author, and marketing consultant.

As an independent composer and producer, he has focused on music for film and television, including trailers, promos, underscore, and advertising. His music for television promos has been heard for the NBC hit series *Smash* as well as *The Apprentice*—and most recently for the NBC series *Who Do You Think You Are?*, a Hollywood Music in Media Awards (HMMA) winner for Original Score, TV Promo. He also received an award from the Hollywood Reporter/Billboard Film and TV Music Conference for Best Music Trailer in the Video Games Category for the game *Saints & Sinners*.

Robert's music for reality television shows includes *Dance War, American Idol, Cheer,* and numerous other cues for ABC, FOX, the Biography Channel, BET, the Discovery Channel, the Learning Channel, Spike TV, and the CW.

Robert also founded Track Record Studios in Los Angeles, where he produced tracks for The Association, Canned Heat, and Chad Stuart, and he engineered for Brian Wilson and Fleetwood Mac.

As an author, Robert wrote *Make Your Music Video and Put It Online* for Cengage Learning. He also served as staff writer for *Keyboard* magazine, as well as writing articles for other industry pubs, such as *Mix* magazine, *Songwriter, Cue, The Hollywood Reporter,* and *The Score*, a publication of the Society of Composers and Lyricists (SCL), a highly respected industry organization.

As a panelist, Robert has presented at the Computer Game Developer's Conference, AES (Audio Engineering Society), Mix '99, and California Lawyers for the Arts.

Robert's marketing expertise has been utilized by companies such as Microsoft, Avid (Digidesign), E-MU Systems, Akai, JBL Professional, Aureal, and Cisco Systems.

Contents

Chapter 5
Marketing Your Music the Traditional Way   39

Chapter 6
Leveraging Social Marketing Techniques   51

Chapter 7
Music and Merchandising   71

Chapter 8
The Aesthetics of Developing Merchandise   75

Chapter 9
Other Business Considerations of Music Merchandising   87

Chapter 10
Latest Trends in Digital Music   93

Chapter 15
Conclusions, Musings, and Reminders

191

Introduction

Sometimes books have catchy titles. Other times, they simply state very clearly what the book is about. This is one of those titles—very straightforward, no mystery as to the topic at hand. But because of the alliteration of the M's in those three words, I like to refer to the book as M3. Besides, it's shorter—and we all know how many seconds per day we can save by using acronyms rather than saying the full word.

But I also have a problem with the word "merchandising." Perhaps it's not a problem; maybe it's just a quirk. But every time I hear that word, I think of *Spaceballs*, the 1987 Mel Brooks movie. It's a parody of movies such as *Star Wars, Star Trek*, as well as a few others thrown in for good measure, such as *The Wizard of Oz*.

Here's an excerpt of dialog from the film's script. To appreciate this quirky problem of mine, make sure you read the word "merchandising" the way that Mel Brooks said it in the movie—not "merchandising," but "moichandising."

Lone Starr: But Yogurt, what *is* this place? What is it that you do here?

Yogurt: Moichandising.

Barf: Merchandising? What's that?

Yogurt: Moichandising! Come, I'll show you. *[To the Dinks]* Open up this door. *[Yogurt walks over to a wall filled with* Spaceballs *merchandise.]*

Yogurt: Heh-heh. Come! We put the picture's name on everything! *[Everyone is staring in amazement]*

Yogurt: Moichandising! Moichandising! Where the real money from the movie is made. *Spaceballs*: the T-shirt, *Spaceballs*: the coloring book *[holds up a Transformers comic book]*, *Spaceballs*: the lunchbox, *Spaceballs*: the breakfast cereal! *Spaceballs*: the flame thrower! *[Fires a blast from flame thrower]*

Dinks: Ooohh!

Yogurt: The kids love this one. And last, but not least, *Spaceballs*: the Doll—me. *[Yogurt squeezes the doll, which says, "May the Schwartz be with you!"]*

Yogurt: Adorable.

And so it seems that for the rest of my life, the word will never sound the same to me, whether spoken by someone else or simply the voice in my head. If you saw the movie—and it *was* pretty funny—you'll know what I mean. If you haven't seen it, just remember my little quirk. That way, while reading this book, if you ever feel overwhelmed by the topic "music marketing and merchandising for musicians," you can think of the quirky mispronunciation—it's a great stress reliever and a fun way of telling people what you're currently reading.

Note: The word "musician" in this book will often mean musician, songwriter, artist, or composer. These words may be used interchangeably at times, so simply apply whichever one (or ones) are relevant to you.

Regardless of whether you choose to have fun with the title, as a musician, you likely take the topic somewhat seriously. After all, the transition from an analog to a digital world has disrupted the norms of many businesses. This is very evident in the music business, in which technology has enabled songwriters, composers, and musicians to create master-quality recordings in their own homes, reducing the role of traditional record companies.

This do-it-yourself method is now changing the way music is marketed. As is the case with producing music, the marketing, promotion, and merchandising functions are becoming more than a mere trend for musicians; they are becoming a necessity. This book not only deals with the nuts and bolts of these functions, it also puts them in the overall perspective of a musician's career. To put it another way, my intention is to provide you with more than a simple list of tasks for marketing and merchandising of your music—my aim is to provide you with the strategy behind the tactics.

But before we jump headfirst into this swimming pool sometimes referred to as *Music 2.0* or even *Music 3.0*, a word to the wise: This new do-it-yourself, who-needs-a-record-company method is not easy—it's actually very hard. This makes perfect sense. If you're going to do the work that used to be done by A&R executives, music producers, recording engineers, mastering engineers, marketing staff, publicists, tour managers—you get the idea—then you're going to be doing *a lot* of work. Further, just as in the "old" music business, there is no guarantee that any of your hard work is going to pay off. So if you find this proposition scary, it's quite possible that the marketing and merchandising of your own music is not for you. But you already knew that this business wasn't for the weak or timid, didn't you?

If you haven't put this book back on the shelf or returned it to Amazon.com by now, then I guess you're ready for the challenge of facing the brave new world of the new music business. This world was created by a collision of many forces—the transition of analog to digital, of home stereos to portable devices, of albums to one-song digital downloads. The record companies of old didn't see this transition coming—or if they did, they didn't comprehend the impact that these trends would have. Today I read a quote from rapper T-Pain in which he said, "Ain't nobody selling records unless you Susan Boyle," which was his commentary on album sales being incredibly low as well as his considering not releasing music anymore. That's a powerful statement, coming from a recording artist who *does have a record deal*—and getting a record deal was the holy grail of Music 1.0.

Whether T-Pain abandons the traditional record label and becomes a do-it-yourself, independent, new music marketer of the 21st century remains to be seen. But for the rest of you who aren't on a record label, the choice is clearer. The new music business—the new way of doing things—at least provides some hope.

Who Should Read This Book

You should read this book if:

- You're serious about a career in music.

- You're confused about what's going on in the music business.

- You're good at making music but need to get up to speed on technologies such as the Internet, social networking, portable devices, and so on.

- You're good at making music but need to get up to speed on marketing and merchandising your music.

- You understand traditional marketing but haven't quite grasped social marketing.

- You've grasped social marketing but don't quite understand traditional marketing.

- You think there's nothing new to learn about the current state of the music business.

- You want to be prepared for your next career move.

Who Should Not Read This Book

You should *not* read this book if:

- You think the music business is easily understandable.

- You think the music business is static, unchanging, and controllable.

- You don't think marketing plays an important part in your musical career.

- You've thumbed through the book and not one concept seems new to you.

- You are planning to download it illegally and think no one will catch you.

Okay, maybe no one *will* catch you. But that's something you have to live with—and reconcile with the idea that you don't want people illegally downloading *your* music.

A Postscript to the Introduction

I spent a lot of time thinking about the content for this book after I began writing the first chapter. I began to think, "Why would anybody need another book on this topic? There are plenty of such books out there right now." The more I wrote, the more I realized that I wasn't about to simply duplicate the same ideas, regurgitate the same topics, and recycle what many people in the music business already knew. My intent became clear: to apply my own music business experience—good or bad—to each issue or subject matter. Sure, I would drill down to a certain level of detail, but I felt it was more important to put the transition to this new music business in perspective than to write a white paper on Music 3.0.

So, for example, I will discuss downloading music, but I won't get into megabytes, gigabytes, and file-format conversions. I'll discuss websites, but there are probably thousands of books on websites, so I'll cover how to utilize your website as a music marketing tool. I'll cover marketing strategies—both the old and the new—but with an emphasis on how to use which strategy at which time, or when to use one marketing tactic over another. I'll talk about merchandising, but not about what Proctor & Gamble use in their merchandising strategies—I'll talk about merchandising for the 21st-century musician and the things you can accomplish with a do-it-yourself process.

My hope is that this approach is what will keep the book interesting and fresh—and I hope that, as a reader, you will find it that way, too.

1 An Ode to the Record Business

Blame it all on Thomas Edison. If it were not for his invention of the phonograph, perhaps your life would be simpler. Sure, you could play music to your heart's content, but without a way of distributing it—of providing other humanoids with a means of hearing your masterpieces—you wouldn't be constantly yearning to be heard. Of course, the phonograph *was* invented, and now you have to rise to the occasion. Get your music heard or forever be known as a hobbyist, a weekender, a wannabe....

Thomas Alwa Edison.

So, you want to be a rock 'n roll star? Before I go too far, I would like to engage in a little history lesson. In this chapter, I will take you on a tour of what the music industry once was. Then the bus will stop at what the music industry currently is. By virtue of fact-finding and deductive reasoning, I will look ahead to what the music industry is becoming. Finally, and most importantly, I will try to help you figure out what all of this means to you.

We need to do this before we do anything else. You've probably heard the saying by philosopher George Santayana: "Those who cannot remember the past are condemned to repeat it."

What the Music Industry Once Was

When I think of the word "industry," I think of factories, smokestacks, machinery, hot metal, and burning coals. So why do they call it the music *industry*? (And who are "they," anyway?)

The music business came of age in the industrialized 20th century. It became an economically viable entity in which factories (record companies) produced a physical product (vinyl recordings, tapes, CDs) to be consumed by the public (me, you, our ancestors, friends, relatives, and several billion other people). It became like, well, an industry.

But wait a minute: Don't industries consist of huge conglomerates, headed by cigar-smoking businessmen who put profits before people and who really do not have their customers' interests at heart? Did the music industry of old really fit that image? Well, in a word, yes. But like most things,

Figure 1.1 The early days of radio. AM radio was the key to getting a hit (although this particular photo may pre-date your image of what an AM radio station looked like).

it may have started off in one way and ended up in another. I can say this, because I was there in the "early days." I remember when the music industry was a sweet little baby. I remember the thrill of playing 45 rpm and 78 rpm records by the Drifters, the Everly Brothers, Dion and the Belmonts, and Ritchie Valens. Heck, I remember playing surf music by Dick Dale and the Deltones, not to mention Duane Eddy! All of this was before the Beatles, and I remember them, too!

It was a magical time. A time of innocence. A time of consequences. And yes, I remember Simon and Garfunkel, too.

It's important to consider some of music business history because it gives vital clues as to how we got to where we are today. In the early days, record companies were all-powerful, and AM radio was the key star-power through the release of singles. (See Figure 1.1.)

These stars may have been one-hit wonders, but most had long-term relationships with producers and A&R (Artist & Repertoire) staff at the label, thus creating an environment in which an artist could develop. AM radio made money through numerous commercial sponsors, record companies through multiple avenues of sales and royalties, and local music stores through the sale of hit singles and albums. Beyond this, record companies, promoters, and radio stations engaged in the practice of payola—illegal methods of kickbacks and bribes used to get certain records played on the air.

A major renaissance occurred in the late '60s with the emergence of FM radio. With barely any commercial interruptions whatsoever, FM stations would play entire albums, beginning to end. The radio announcers had deep, mellow voices—or perhaps it just seemed that way because for the first time, you could hear the full audio spectrum, including the low frequencies, over the air. It was both exciting and soothing. And music, not commercials, ruled the airwaves. The industry was driven by those wearing jeans and T-shirts—until ultimately, certain people smelled money, and the suits arrived. Now the music didn't matter, as long as it was music that made money. Soon, FM radio sounded more like Top 40 radio—consisting of limited playlists that repeated over and over. The days of album cuts were over. Accountants and lawyers took over the reins from hippies and dreamers. Many record companies ultimately merged into a handful of conglomerates. And the beat goes on.

All along, record-company executives were extremely paranoid of "illegal" copying of music. They protested the cassette recorder. Then they had a fit over DAT (*Digital Audio Tape*) recorders—even though most record-company executives had DAT recorders in their own offices. They were glad that consumers loved CDs, so they charged accordingly. At first, they told us the high prices of CDs were necessary because the CD was such a new medium—and that after a short time, with more and more CD production, the prices would come down. Funny, that never happened. (See Figure 1.2.) And so, consumers bought more and more expensive CDs that usually had one or two cuts they really liked. Artist royalties didn't increase, but record-company profits did. Something about all of this seemed inherently unfair.

Figure 1.2 Consumers bought stacks of CDs—but prices never went down.

Where the Music Industry Is

First, I would like to make one thing very clear. I am against the illegal downloading, copying, and distribution of music without the artists' consent. I am a believer in copyright ownership and artists' rights. On one hand, it is a moral issue; on the other, it is a very practical matter of artists being able to make a living. Some people think that the word "stealing" is too harsh when it comes to illegal downloading. I disagree. It is no different from me coming into your home and taking something that belongs to you. Worse yet, and a better analogy, would be me coming into your home and taking an original painting of yours that took years to create. I would be stealing and violating your creative rights, all at the same time.

Having said that, I can clearly see why this practice has become a problem. If you take a close look at the "What the Music Industry Once Was" section, you can see the basic rules of cause and effect coming into play. For a quick review, here are some of the causes:

- Record companies holding onto their assets with clenched fists, disallowing reasonable or "fair use" of music copying for personal enjoyment

- Record companies ripping off customers with exorbitant CD prices while promising that one day CDs would become more affordable—but never delivering on that promise

- Record companies, in collusion with pop radio, severely limiting the variety of music on the radio, while simultaneously preventing truly good talent from making it to the top

- Record companies charging emerging artists with hugely marked-up recording and promotional costs, making it difficult (if not impossible) for those artists to ever break even, let alone make a profit

- Record companies, in compliance with publishing companies, taking over ownership, copyright, and publishing of artists' material without any intention of leveraging that material elsewhere and never allowing the artist or songwriter reversion rights (in which, after a number of years, the rights are returned to the creator of the music if nothing else has happened with the material)

You can see an arc of injustice that includes everyone from the consumer to the creator, with the record company insulated from all of it, not to mention *causing* all of it. It's enough to make you want to rebel. And that's exactly what's happened.

The fall of the Great Record Empire was caused by a perfect storm. All of the causes listed here, plus the record companies' refusal to see the writing on the wall—namely, the effect of the Internet on music distribution—contributed to this storm.

As the clouds clear, we are left with two sea changes. Consumers are no longer willing to pay big bucks (and some aren't will to pay *anything*) for albums that may contain a couple of good songs. Second, musicians, including artists and songwriters, are no longer tied to the goal of reaching the big record deal in the sky. As such, artists have to take on all of the tasks that the record company used to do.

What the Music Business Is Becoming

Anyone who knows *exactly* what the music business is becoming, with a high degree of accuracy, should be writing a business plan instead of reading this book. Looking at the history of the business as well as current trends can suggest possible futures, with *possible* being the key word.

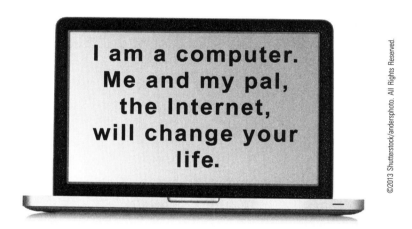

Without a doubt, the Internet is the enabler, the catalyst, and the vehicle for the largest change in music business history, outside of the original phonograph. Although we now recognize the computer as a distribution platform for all types of media, nobody had a clue about this at first. Digital music files, especially when reduced in size by the MP3 format, are easily distributed through the Internet. They are also easily downloaded and may be shared by peer-to-peer networks. Thus was the beginning of services such as MP3.com and Napster, companies that took advantage of technology but without any regard to copyright. Record companies stood by and watched for a long time, without believing that there was much credibility in digital distribution and sharing methods. But after a time, with the copyright issues challenged in court, illegal downloading came to a halt.

The story would end here if it were not for the launch of Apple's iTunes. The business model for iTunes, as well as the invention of the iPod and other portable devices, was and still is a great

Source: Apple and iTunes.

Figure 1.3 The Beatles are truly a boost to Apple and to Beatles fans with their music added to the iTunes music inventory.

success. These products, introduced in the 2001 to 2003 timeframe, finally legitimized and monetized the digital downloading of music. Record labels came on board reluctantly (surprised?), and yet iTunes has expanded to include music videos, movies, television shows, videogames, podcasts, and just recently the Beatles were added to the iTunes repertoire. (Talk about coming full circle—see Figure 1.3.)

The iTunes model allowed for the return to singles, which makes sense because most people hear, react to, and want to obtain a particular song they've heard. The single sells for an average price of $1.29 (although some are more or less than that). Record companies have never been big fans of this pricing scheme and business model, but you'd think after all the decades of wrong moves and bad decisions, the industry would want to course-correct and do the right things. Nevertheless, they have migrated to what is known as the *360 Deal*. In this model, the record company attempts to make money off of every conceivable revenue stream that the artist has—including touring, publishing, and merchandising. You can imagine that this idea is not going over very well, and in fact is having the same effect that all record company decisions have had over the years—artists are heading for the hills, shouting, "We don't need no stinkin' record deal."

What This Means to You

And thus we land here, in the present, where FUD (fear, uncertainty, and doubt) are some of the driving factors of the new music business. Fear underscores the record companies' very existence, uncertainty is guiding the careers of today's recording artists, and doubt is ever present everywhere.

The trick is to allow the uncertainty to exist, but not allow it to stop your career. There is evidence everywhere of artists that still bubble to the surface, each of them with a slightly different roadmap that has led to their success. Notice that I didn't say "formula" for success, for there is no formula now, and there really wasn't one before.

Nevertheless, there are things you can do to market yourself in the music business that were unheard of before and certainly would not be possible without the digital age of the Internet. Those are some of the things I will explore in the rest of this book, but unlike some other books of the "Music 2.0" genre, I will not throw out the baby with the bathwater. I will give you lots of tools that come under the category of "traditional" marketing techniques, as well as ideas and methods for creating your own merchandise.

So, it's a DIY (do-it-yourself) adventure, and that means it's up to you to DIY.

2 Becoming the New Musician

Throughout my years in the music business, I've been constantly surprised by some of the assumptions that artists make about their futures. Perhaps their vision is clouded by the intoxicating smell of stardom. Or maybe they think that the world is basically fair, and if you have good intentions, good things will happen to you. Overriding all of this is the misconception that if you have enough talent, you will "make it" in the business. As you well know, none of this is true. (You *did* know that, didn't you?)

Some misunderstandings about the way things work can be attributed to lack of experience and knowledge. Other misconceptions are due to the "new way" in which things are being done in the digital-powered music business. I will attempt to sort through some of these.

Isn't Having Talent Enough?

I'm sure *you* didn't pose this question—I'm just addressing this to all of the other emerging artists who don't know the answer to this. *You*, obviously, are way beyond this simple assumption. So just hang with me while I explain to everybody else, okay?

The short answer, of course, is *no*. Having talent is *not* enough.

If you lined up all of the potential recording artists who had the ability and talent to make it, but who lacked some of the other ingredients, they would form a line that would circle the earth 1,819 times. How do I know this figure? I don't. But you get the idea.

Was Lana Turner really discovered while sitting at the soda fountain at Schwab's Drugstore in Hollywood? No one knows for sure, but this legendary tale may be, in part, why up-and-coming artists think they will be discovered. The only organization that is going to discover *you* is the IRS, if you owe back taxes. Or perhaps a telemarketer when you've just sat down to dinner. But entertainment agents, managers, and producers? Not likely. So don't go to Schwab's—not only is it no longer there, it's simply a bad strategy.

The most difficult task for any artist is to be objective about himself and his music. I witnessed this way too many times when musicians came into my recording studio to record demos. No matter how good—or how bad—the music was on the good/bad continuum, all artists thought they were the next best thing after Elvis, the Beatles, or now, Lady Gaga. But you've likely seen

Figure 2.1 You can no longer get discovered at Schwab's, although an industrious person might create a "Virtual Schwab's" online for finding talent (and send me a check, please).

this as well. If you haven't, just tune into the *American Idol* auditions, and you'll see what I mean.

Please don't send letters telling me how insensitive I am to the emotional needs of recording artists such as yourself. I actually understand this very well. There is an indescribable satisfaction to writing, performing, and recording your own music. It is heightened the more you perfect your craft. It's not a job; it's a calling. You have to do it. You can't—and won't—do anything else. You'd just as soon crawl into a hole—probably the one in the middle of your guitar—and disappear before you'd give up on your music. I get it. I understand. It's what drives you, motivates you, makes you who you are. And maybe, just maybe, you have the talent to back this up. So, are having this talent and this drive enough? Sorry, Charlie. The answer, once again, is no.

Never-ending perseverance, fortitude, and the ability to withstand rejection—all of the qualities that are part of what is necessary to survive in this business—still hold true. But with the music business becoming something different than it used to be, there are other qualities, as well as other responsibilities, that go with it. Your role as an artist, as it used to be defined, is changing, and this role requires you to do new things that you likely never dreamed of doing.

Your Role as an Artist

You are now a person who must wear many hats. You must be a jack-of-all-trades, master of most.

Director   Producer

Indiana Jones   Musician

IRS Agent   Songwriter

Perhaps the biggest change the Internet has brought to the music business is the ability to have direct communication between artist and fan. Whether or not you believe in this new model is almost beside the point. Because this type of interaction is a reality, your potential fan base is already aware of the possibilities—and their expectations are that you support this idea as well. So, the fact that you don't have a marketing staff and publicists doesn't come into play. *You* are the marketing staff and publicist.

It's also important to understand that the communication is *two-way* communication, and to that extent, the "marketing staff and publicist" idea is not a perfect analogy. True, you will market and promote yourself. But the old rules of how this is done may no longer apply.

Defining, developing, and nurturing a fan base is the new record promotion of today. Whether you are an indie heavy metal band or a new string quartet doesn't matter—you need to find your audience, and they need to find you. I will get into the details of how this is done in subsequent chapters, especially Chapter 4, "Knowing Your Audience"—the intent of *this* chapter is to introduce you to the concept and prepare you for the inevitable. The days of "I just wanna make music" are over—that is, if you want to seriously create music for a living. You are no longer just an artist. You are the complete package—and the responsibility for your success as an artist largely relies upon you.

Does the Record Company Have a Role?

This is a burning question on the minds of many people in the music business. What's going to happen to the record companies? If we all admit that they missed opportunities created by the transition to the digital age and the Internet, what's going to become of them from this point forward?

The strength of the record companies was their ability to invest in, nurture, and expose new talent. Of those functions, the first one—investing—is the most critical and valuable to an emerging artist. In this regard, record companies were like banks—or more accurately, investment banks. The digital revolution has created other routes to the marketplace, and in this regard, the relevancy of record companies is diminished.

Another consideration in answering this question lies in your definition of success. The do-it-yourself artist can accomplish tremendous things by wearing the different hats discussed a moment ago. But can a DIY, homegrown, independent musician achieve the kind of success of, say, Beyoncé? And further, does it matter? For many independent musicians, the ability to do what they love and make a living at it is enough. Where are you on this question? The answer is critical to your career choices and also speaks to the core question of this section—does a record company have a role?

Here is one example of which way the trend is going. Recently, YouTube announced a new program called *Musicians Wanted*. The Google-owned site offers independent musicians the

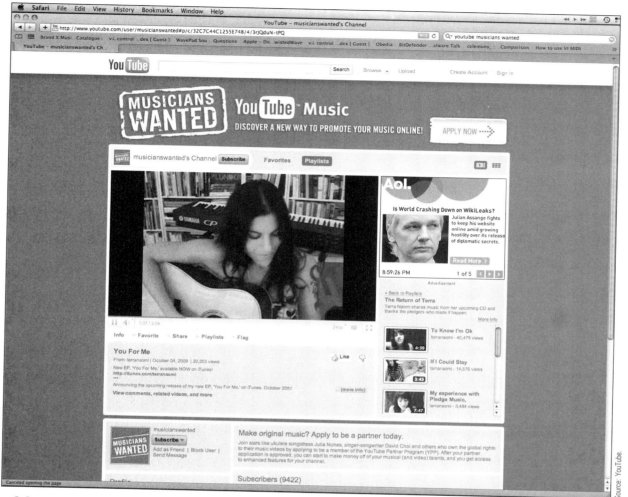

Figure 2.2 You don't need to be a superstar to get onto YouTube's Musicians Wanted page.

opportunity to create a homepage or channel and share in the ad revenues generated by their videos. Until now, YouTube only offered the revenue-sharing option to artists who have contracts with record labels or who have special contracts with the video-sharing site. Think about that for a minute. Up until now, you had to have a major record deal to qualify. Now, if you've got original music and can make a decent music video (and here is a plug for my other book, *Make Your Music Video and Put it Online* [Course Technology PTR, 2010]), you can make music videos, post them on your own YouTube channel, and hopefully, make some money doing it. You don't need to be a record company or be signed to one in order to qualify. This is just another indication of how things are changing.

The Psychology and Morality of Buying Music

Because this chapter finds us at the unique intersection of the "old" music business transforming into its new, digital counterpart, it would make sense to address a phenomenon that affects all artists, record companies, and music fans. This is about a rallying cry among certain groups of people that "Music should be free." The Internet has created a monster of sorts. It is the notion that "if I can get it, then I don't have to pay for it." Of course, you could be a jewel thief and make the same statement, but that doesn't make it right.

The sad part is that this group has been so vocal that songwriters and artists are caving into the idea. "Well, if it has to be free, I'll have to make money selling T-shirts." Hold on, fella! The conversation has just begun.

The rationalizations among the "free" crowd are numerous:

■ Record labels sold us lousy CDs with only two good songs on them.

■ Record companies are greedy corporations.

■ The Internet has made copying easy, so we should therefore be allowed to copy.

■ I'm not paying for ownership, just access—and on the Internet, access is free.

■ It's too late, file sharing is a reality—artists need to find other ways to make money.

The list goes on. These cries are often delivered in an angry, adolescent tone of voice. The polarization of the free versus pay crowd has become as extreme as the political scene in the United States today.

The problem with extremes is that they leave no gray areas, and on this topic, there are a lot of gray areas.

Because it is so easy to create and distribute music, its value has been called into question. There is no scarcity of artists or songwriters in the business; actually, there is an overabundance of them. With overabundance come the rules of supply and demand, yet there is no "physical" product that we're dealing with, so what exactly are we measuring? If it's the intellectual property value of the music, then the "physical-ness" doesn't matter. We paid for music on vinyl, tape, and CDs—so now it's in digital format. So what? Does that make it any less valuable?

We must ask the "free" crowd where the line is drawn. Is all digital content free for the taking? Music, books, film, video, television, art—anything at all as long as it's in a digital format?

The "pay" crowd—in particular, the artists—has already acquiesced to a degree by resorting to other means of making money to make up for the lack of income generated by music sales. Now, let's face it—this book is about this very topic. How can you use marketing and merchandising techniques to increase your revenue as an artist? Yes, that is something we are all interested in doing. But at the expense of making your music free? As I will point out from time to time in other parts of the book, "free" can be used as part of a promotional strategy; "free" as a price point amounts to a failed business model.

Stealing is stealing. And record companies did not gain any fans by suing those who engaged in file sharing or illegal downloading of music. These are extremes. The successful formula for making and selling music will emerge, but it's going to take more time. In the meantime, you have to find a middle ground where you're not giving your music away all of the time.

Figure 2.3 Does the value of music fade away as we journey further into the digital era? Let's hope not.

Each time you engage in activities in which you give something for nothing, music becomes devalued—not only for you, but for everyone else as well.

How You Contribute to the "Music Is Free" Idea

The value of music is declining rapidly, day by day. Artists are well aware of the difficulty of becoming noticed among the huge crowd of emerging artists. The need to rise above the "noise floor" is so strong that in many cases, musicians are willing to give away their music, no questions asked. You might think that this is due to the effects that the Internet has had on the music business, and to some extent you'd be right. But has it always been this way? In a word, yes. The history of the music business has always confused the value of music itself with the need to monetize and profit from it.

Pray to Play

The challenge for an artist to rise to the top in the "old" music business was never an easy task. But the mechanics of how an artist went from being unknown to a superstar were mostly invisible, or at the very best, magical. An artist would compose, write, play live, tour, compose, write, play, and so on, hoping to get "discovered." Essentially, you had to pray that something would happen to ignite your career. You had to Pray to Play. As the music business flourished from the 1960s to, say, the 1990s, artists learned more about the craft of songwriting (using hooks, proper song structure, and so on) while more and more independent record labels joined the gold rush.

Still, the formula for getting your act on the Top 40 or Top 100 or Top 200 remained the same. Pray to Play.

Pay to Play

Pay to Play has two distinct meanings. The first one has to do with "payola." Although the process of how hit songs became hit songs was largely unknown to the general public, insiders knew that many methods were illegal or, at the very best, unethical. Publishers, promoters, and record companies were not averse to paying radio stations under the table to play particular records, giving them an unfair advantage over those who played by the rules. This practice was common back in the late 1950s and continued over time until it became exposed, although it still continued on a smaller scale. The music business was very competitive, and in many cases, if you wanted to get heard, you had to Pay to Play.

Fast forward to today. The Internet has supposedly "democratized" the music business so that virtually anyone has a chance to make it. The significance of payola in the business has lost its meaning along with the importance of radio and record companies in general (although I would hesitate to dismiss their significance entirely). So where does Pay to Play come in?

The Internet is rife with websites for musicians to upload their music. Some are:

■ Music libraries that are available for producers, film and television directors, and other licensors of music to explore and select music for specific opportunities. They usually charge up-front licensing fees and may or may not split them 50/50 with the music creator. They will usually stress that the songwriter will benefit from performance royalties from PROs (*performing rights organizations*), such as ASCAP and BMI, after the proper cue sheets are filed by the production company and submitted to the PRO.

■ "Matchmakers" that present music job opportunities online and charge a fee to the subscribers (read: musicians, artists, composers) who submit material. The artist or songwriter may be required to pay an annual subscription fee or pay fees with each submission, or both. Usually, it's both.

■ "Opportunity engines" that function as online A&R (*artist and repertoire*) departments, finding and exposing talent to the right music seekers, taking a percentage of the artist's profits for doing so. Not every artist or band will be plugged into opportunities. Many will be referred to partners of the online A&R website and will be offered discounts on other goods or services.

Not every artist will have her music automatically approved for any of these scenarios. In almost every case, these companies screen the submitted music and determine whether the music is qualified. There are some cases in which the music is screened by a machine. They may not have a staff that reviews submitted material, but they have a computer with algorithms that knows a hit song when it "hears" it. (No, I am *not* kidding.)

Music libraries impose the least amount of risk and cost to the artist. If you sign your music with them—either on an exclusive or nonexclusive basis—and it gets used, you get paid your performance royalties (and possibly some share of the licensing fees that the library charges its customers). It's rare that you would be charged a submission fee or subscription fee, although there are some online music libraries that do so. You Pay to Play.

Sites that post music opportunities may charge you a subscription fee and/or a fee for each song that you submit for that opportunity. You Pay to Play.

Opportunity engines will take a piece of your action, if and when your submission is used. You Pay to Play.

There are variations on these themes or business models. The amount of success that is promised by these companies covers the gamut and varies widely by the copywriting ability of their respective marketing departments. The amount of new "opportunity" companies that appear every week on the Internet is growing exponentially. (I don't know if the figure is actually an exponent of some sort, but everyone always says "exponentially," so why can't I?)

And now, ladies and gentlemen, the disclaimer:

I'M NOT SAYING THAT THESE COMPANIES ARE ILLEGITIMATE, UNETHICAL, OR OTHERWISE DETRIMENTAL. THEY VARY ACCORDING TO WHAT THEY CHARGE AND WHAT THEY CAN ACTUALLY DO FOR YOU. SOME ARE MOTIVATED BY THE LOVE OF MUSIC, SOME BY PROFIT, SOME BY GREED, OR ANY COMBINATION THEREOF. IT IS UP TO YOU TO FILTER THROUGH THEM AND DETERMINE WHICH, IF ANY, OF THESE COMPANIES OFFER AN OPPORTUNITY FOR YOU TO EXPOSE YOUR MUSIC.

There, I said it. (I wasn't shouting, by the way. Disclaimers are often written in all CAPS on contracts—and I also wanted to catch your attention.)

By now, you might be wondering what any of this has to do with how you contribute to the "music is free" idea. Read on.

Music Is Not Born Free—But It Is Available at No Cost

The explosion of music creators, music libraries, music licensing companies, and other related entities is phenomenal in its rate of expansion and inversely proportional to the available music opportunities. What did I just say? In everyday language, there are a helluva lot more people trying to place music and make money from it than there are ways to do so. Don't think about this too much—you'll get depressed.

What is more disturbing than this reality is how some people have taken advantage of it. Although it is natural for prices to be driven down in a market in which there's more supply than demand, it is difficult to do so when dealing with creative material that has its own intellectual property value—as opposed to products such as soap, screwdrivers, and widgets. There are intangible, subjective, and otherwise difficult-to-measure qualities in a piece of original music. There is also a huge variable in value according to how the music will be used. The hardware store doesn't care what you do with your screwdriver.

Because music users are very aware of what the marketplace is like these days, some whittle down the price of music to zero—that is, they will offer you the "opportunity" to use your music without paying you a cent. While most people in a level-headed state of mind might consider this ridiculous, when it comes to music anything goes. The overabundance of musicians, artists, and songwriters creates an atmosphere in which music creators are sometimes *desperate* for recognition. Granted, there is a certain logic to the idea that if you offered a piece of music for free to a film director, television producer, or other opportunity, there would likely be more opportunities in the future for which you *might* be paid. Read again: *might* be paid. The more likely scenario is that you *won't* be paid. The psychology of the music user is "If I got it for free before, why should I pay now?" Sound familiar? It's very much like the Internet user who is into file sharing and illegal downloading. "If I got it for free before, why should I pay now?"

The idea of providing music for free does have its place when used as a promotional tool, which I'll discuss in more detail in Chapters 7, 8, and 10. But the discussion here is about providing cost-free, licensing-free, no-strings-attached music in a business transaction. This practice is not healthy and may have harmful effects to your long-term career. But do you know who the biggest culprit is?

YOU. Okay, maybe not you personally, but the general you—people *like* you—your colleagues, friends, competitors, and other players in the music business who go along with the idea that it's okay to give music away for free. The number of people creating music is increasing, the consumers of music are devaluing what music is worth, and the music-for-free providers are increasing the rate of decline while simultaneously forcing the value of music even lower. This is a losing formula.

So the way you contribute to the music-is-free idea—or at the very least, the devaluation of music in general—is by being a willing participant in any business transaction in which you give your music away for free. What is difficult for many suppliers of music to comprehend (or suppliers of any sort, for that matter) is that their actions actually have an effect on the overall market-place. That means *you*. Consider what you are willing to do to get your music played—and even more, what effect this might have on the music market in general.

The notion that your actions as an individual can have an effect on millions of people or trends or accepted ideas may sound corny or otherwise insignificant—like recycling did when you first heard about it. By the way, recycling *has* proven to work and help the environment. Now you can do things to help your own work environment. Don't throw *your* product into the trash.

Figure 2.4 Every single decision you make can affect millions of others, much in the same way that recycling has affected the environmental health of the whole planet.

3 Understanding Marketing Terminology

As you will see throughout this book, many marketing concepts have both old and new definitions. That fact, in and of itself, tells you how much things have changed in the last couple of decades. At the very least, even if many of the core definitions are quite similar, the way they are implemented is quite different.

The essence of this difference lies in one word—interactivity. The world of music marketing is a two-way street that requires audience involvement, input, and action. So, for example, whereas marketing used to mean a "push" type of action that began with messages that traveled from the corporation (read: music business or *any* business) to the consumer, marketing today comprehends, appreciates, values, and incorporates messages from the consumer as well.

Definitions: Traditional Marketing

Here are some broad-brush definitions of the words that are integral to the traditional marketing process. I will get into more detail on these and other marketing topics in Chapters 4 and 5.

- **Marketing.** Marketing is defined as the strategy behind the activities you use to get your product, company, band, record, or service noticed by customers or prospective customers. You use marketing techniques to identify your customer or target market. Once you've done that, you identify their needs or expectations and fulfill them more effectively than your competition. Your approach or technique for marketing is based on a marketing strategy. The specific things you do to execute on your strategy are your marketing tactics.

- **Merchandising.** Merchandising is the most commercial form of marketing. Merchandising might imply the packaging of your product to a point-of-sale display in a retail store. Merchandising could mean selling T-shirts and coffee mugs with your logo on it to campaigns that tie you or your product together with a celebrity or television show or motion picture. As you can see, merchandising involves the nitty-gritty details of marketing, yet it spans a wide range of activities on a tactical level.

- **Promotion.** Promotion is composed of the things you do to influence or otherwise persuade a customer or potential customer's buying decision. Promotion may utilize traditional media, such as television, radio, or newspapers, with a very specific goal in mind—increasing awareness of a product or service and hence the demand for that product or service.

- **Publicity.** Publicity is another means of influencing an audience but is usually more factual or news-based, rather than advertising, which is bought and paid for. Publicity may mean landing a news story about you or your product, sponsoring an event, or organizing a press tour. Publicity and PR (*public relations*) are words that are often used interchangeably to mean the same thing.

- **Branding.** Branding is the process of creating and reinforcing a personality or image of a product or service. The brand is ultimately the *perception* of your product that a customer or prospect forms and retains in his or her mind. Branding is so elaborate that it has spawned a dozen subcategories, such as brand name, brand image, brand equity, brand loyalty, and brand extension. If you do your branding successfully, then you will create brand recognition, which usually is a positive, memorable perception of your product.

- **Integrated marketing.** Integrated marketing unifies different marketing approaches into a consistent and ongoing marketing program. It may, for example, combine mass marketing with direct marketing and viral marketing. The idea is to maximize marketing strategy by taking advantage of the relative strength of each approach in combination, rather than individually.

- **360-degree marketing.** This is a holistic marketing approach that looks at all the "touch points" around the customer. It is a "customer-centric" point of view that may include online, broadcast, and print campaigns, all designed to create a story around the customer and ultimately engage him or her in a long-term relationship with your organization or company.

The Marketing Plan

These concepts are just a sample of what might comprise a traditional marketing plan. No matter what type of marketing mix you decide to use, it's vital to come up with a marketing plan. A marketing plan is your written document that provides the details on how you will achieve your marketing goals. A marketing plan can be the bible or roadmap for a product, a service, or your band and its music.

A marketing plan does not have to be a 100-page document that is sure to impress businesspeople or make the faces of your closest friends glaze over in confusion. But I can say this—there is a huge difference between the simplest of marketing plans and the idea that you can carry around a marketing plan in your head. It doesn't work that way. Just the process of writing things down can make a world of difference in your own understanding of your goals. Figure 3.1 demonstrates the most basic of marketing plans—a plan that does not require a degree in marketing to create or understand. They can also be as complex as you want—or anything in between.

Figure 3.2 shows a marketing plan that is more relevant to you as a musician or artist. Of the different categories, *branding* is the one that is most critical, because it will determine much of

Figure 3.1 This basic marketing plan would work for almost any situation.

Figure 3.2 Your music marketing plan should start with a branding exercise—everything else you do will be based upon your brand identity.

the rest of the plan, so that's a good place to start. Keep in mind that all of the categories will have additional "branches" that contain details relevant to those activities.

In the days of the Silicon Valley gold rush (or perhaps I should say *software rush*), marketing plans were written on the backs of napkins and could garner tens of millions of dollars in venture capital funds. Other plans were PowerPoint presentations that consisted of four or five slides. And some other plans were hundreds of pages long. Still, they were written plans—so if you do nothing else, write down everything that comes to mind while making your career roadmap.

Definitions: Social Marketing

Fast forward to today, where social marketing is the "new marketing." Technically, it might be more accurate to say "social media marketing," which, among other things, uses different Internet marketing sites, such as Facebook Twitter, and MySpace, as a means to reach one's target audience (or, more accurately, to *join* one's target audience). The entire phenomenon of social media marketing, from blogging to tweeting, is sometimes grouped under the general heading of "Web 2.0." For the purposes of this book, I will use the terms "social marketing" and "social media marketing" interchangeably, and I will always use it to mean the Web 2.0 (or, to get completely up to date, Web 3.0) phenomenon.

Social media marketing is a much newer phenomenon than traditional marketing or even viral and guerrilla marketing. Sometimes the latest, greatest thing is overly hyped when it first emerges. It remains to be seen whether social media marketing falls into the overhyped category. Time usually tells the difference, and there has not yet been enough time to know one way or another for certain. Thus, my discussion of social media marketing comes with a cautionary message to use these new marketing tactics with moderation—unless of course you are creating such a buzz that your ears won't stop ringing. In that case, keep doing what you're doing, without restraint. Overall, social media marketing is viewed as part of an integrated marketing strategy.

Social marketing goes beyond simply visiting popular social websites to include activities such as blogging, posting on forums, creating YouTube or MySpace videos, leaving comments on relative websites, and other actions you can see in Figure 3.3, a rough sketch of a social media marketing plan. I will delve into further details on this in Chapter 6, "Leveraging Social Marketing Techniques."

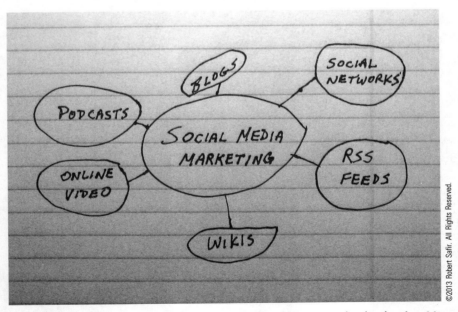

Figure 3.3 Like the previous figures, this social marketing plan covers only the basics. Your plan should drill down much farther, incorporating details for your band or act.

An important thread that you'll see throughout this book is that no single approach to marketing, whether traditional or social, contains all the necessary ingredients to ensure a successful marketing campaign for you as an artist. Further, there is no single formula that reveals precisely the right combination of ingredients *within* traditional or social marketing to ensure success. Each artist carves her own path, utilizing tools and techniques that work for her. It is less important to subscribe to any particular marketing philosophy than it is to execute marketing campaigns that work for you.

4 Knowing Your Audience

If you want to sell the most records (or CDs or downloads or whatever the medium), you might think it logical that you want to appeal to the widest audience possible, right?

Wrong.

You might get *lucky* enough to appeal to the widest audience possible, but that's usually a phenomenon that happens to you, not something that happens by design. Trying to hit the largest possible target market in one fell swoop is like trying to take down an entire forest with a bow and arrow. At least this analogy has a couple of the right words contained within it—target market. And that's what you need to do—you need to target *your* market.

But alas, you say to yourself, "If I do things the right way, my audience will find *me*; I don't have to figure out how to find *them*." Well, there is some truth to that idea, as long as you take it in the correct order—first, figure out how to find your audience, and ultimately, a larger audience will be able to find you.

Defining Your Target Market

Just what is a target market? In your case, it's a group of fans (or potential fans) that is most likely to like your music. They are the people who will buy your CDs, T-shirts, downloads, and coffee mugs.

You need to visualize and get into the mind of your fans as much as possible, getting into as much detail as possible. How old are they? Are they primarily male or female? Where do they live—or is geography not a concern? How much money do they make—or are they so young that what matters most is how much money their parents make?

It used to be that records—as well as a multitude of other products—were targeted to the 18- to 24-year-old demographic. Those days are over. Those 18-year-olds are now 59 or 60 years old—and yes, they're still buying music. Perhaps they're not buying as much music, but they are nevertheless baby boomers who grew up on rock 'n roll, hit singles, and long-playing 33 RPM albums. Are *they* part of your target market? That's what you have to figure out.

You have to consider lifestyles as well as life stages. Attitudes and aptitudes. Technophobes and techno geeks.

Understanding Market Segmentation

Target marketing involves breaking down your market into segments and then focusing your efforts on a few key segments. This will make the promotion, pricing, and delivery of your product much more effective. Target marketing will do much more than that as well—it will help you determine, to a degree, how to arrange your next song.

In a society that is constantly striving to become more politically correct, is it really right to define your audience by analyzing age factors, socioeconomic factors, and ethnic backgrounds? In a word—yes. Yes, if you want to market your music to an audience that wants to hear it and, hopefully, purchase it.

As far as political correctness goes, recently I was looking for an apartment and wanted to know the general age group of the tenants in that particular building. When I asked the property manager about that, I was surprised to find out that it is not only politically incorrect to ask that question, it's downright illegal. Liability issues regarding age discrimination have become so pronounced that you can't even inquire about an age range of potential neighbors without fearing a possible jail sentence. So, I put the question another way: "What would you say most of the residents are listening to on their iPods—Coldplay or James Taylor?" (You might have to ask if they even *own* iPods!)

So, keep discrimination issues in mind if you have some strange plan to broadcast to the public at large how you've segmented your target market. But rest assured, in the cubicles and conference rooms of most companies, marketers are always slicing and dicing their target market into the most measurable pieces that they can, regardless of whether it is politically correct to do so.

When you segment your market, you can develop a profile of your fans or customers. Profiles may ultimately contain descriptions like this:

■ Young people, 18 to 32, who are technologically savvy

■ Middle-aged people who still prefer CDs to downloads

■ Older people who are still listening to their eight-track tapes and have to be motivated to try anything new

If you don't know what eight-track tapes are, then you're not in the older category—so don't worry about it!

Primary Markets, Secondary Markets, and Niches

The process of defining your market requires that you first define yourself. Who do you sound like? What genre does your music fall into? What artists have influenced you?

If you believe that you sound like no one else and are so completely unique and original that you haven't even been influenced by any other music, put down this book and start looking for another job. The biggest mistake you can make is to believe that you don't sound like anyone else at all (and the logic that usually follows is that you will appeal to absolutely everyone). Further, this creates a marketing crisis. When you tell people that your music cannot be described, that you cannot be put in a box, and that you defy categorization, then there's no way to get anyone interested in your music. So forget that notion and try to align yourself with artists, adjectives, and analogies that best describe your music.

The genre that your music falls into is going to appeal to your primary market. Perhaps your specific genre is country music. That means your audience probably likes other country music artists. (Perhaps you should be living and recording in Nashville, although that's not as necessary in these days of Internet connectedness.)

Some country music artists, such as Faith Hill, intentionally want to expand their appeal beyond the core country music category by having other influences in their music, such as pop or rock. By incorporating these elements into their music, they are reaching a potential secondary market in the pop and rock categories. (See Figure 4.1.) Instead of playing in venues that usually host only country artists, Faith Hill would target mainstream concert halls as well. Having this blend of genres makes her a "crossover" artist. Her primary market is country; her secondary market is pop.

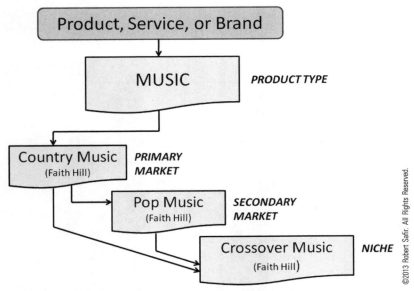

Figure 4.1 You can see the breakdown of primary and secondary markets in this example, featuring Faith Hill, although positioning "Crossover Music" as a niche is a slight overstatement.

If you're lucky, you might find yourself playing in a niche market. A niche market is a focused, targetable portion of a larger market. To be in a niche market means playing in a market segment that no one else "owns" yet. Now, this may seem contrary to what I said earlier about the false belief that you sound like no one else who has come before you. However, even a niche market has its roots in markets that came before it. It is simply more focused and fresh and has a slightly new and original twist to it. These traits have to be balanced with what is accessible, acceptable, and appealing to the market itself. It's a balancing act—be too wide, and you appeal to no one; be too narrow, and you appeal to no one as well.

How Target Marketing Affects Promotion

Your first goal after defining your audience is to determine how to market to that audience effectively. Some of the things that will come into play as a result of your segmentation efforts will be:

- What your logo (if you have one) might look like
- What the album art should look like

- What colors should be used in the artwork and on your website
- The look and feel of your website
- The UI (*user interface*) and navigation style on your website
- What cities you choose for a road tour
- Your style of writing in everything you publish and in the lyrics that you write
- The aesthetic of your MySpace page, Facebook page, and Tweeting style
- The style of artwork on your T-shirts, posters, coffee mugs, mailing labels, and so on

Figure 4.2 shows an example of how a band called "the minimalists" might create their name (and font), their logo, and their album art.

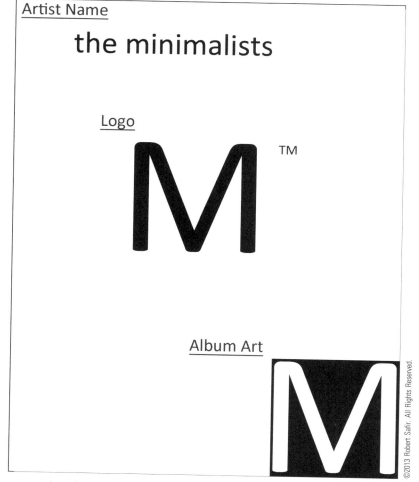

Figure 4.2 Here is an example of a simple concept. This group wouldn't likely use busy artwork, like you might find on the cover of *Sgt. Pepper's Lonely Hearts Club Band*.

You probably get the idea by now. If you don't, try this: Begin with the end in mind. Be the audience. As a fan, what are you thinking? What are you doing? Who else, and what else, do you follow or like? Become a fan of yourself and describe who you are. This is simply another way to look at it.

Knowing Your Fan Base

The new music business requires that you develop and care for your fan base. In days of old, when record companies were in charge of every aspect of your career, an artist was one step removed from her fan base. Fans were people who showed up at your concerts, through little effort of your own, and bought your CDs and other merchandise. An artist did not have to build a fan base on a one-on-one basis. Of course, there were very limited ways to do so even if you wanted to. I'm talking here about the days before social media marketing. Today, understanding and building a fan base is an entirely different matter.

Understanding Your Core and Casual Audiences

Your fan base consists of two primary factions—your core audience and your casual audience. Your core audience is made up of your diehard, passionate fans—those who can't live without your music, thrive on every tidbit of news about you or your band, and know tiny bits of trivia about your act that even you might not know. Your core audience will buy your music, T-shirts, and whatever else you have to sell—as well as recruit other people to become your fans. They can't live without you—but you can't live without them, either.

Your casual audience is not as fanatic. They might like your genre of music. They may even like you—they're just not as passionate or fanatic about it. In an ideal world, you would want to "convert" your casual audience into your core audience. This can happen as part of a natural process, or it can be helped along by your own marketing efforts.

Whether you are talking about your core audience or your casual audience, the truth remains that they need "care and feeding" if you want them to stick around and remain loyal. It is through the processes made available by Web 2.0 that this is able to happen. Those processes include blogs and social networking sites, such as MySpace, Facebook, Twitter, and a host of others, which I'll cover in detail in Chapter 6, "Leveraging Social Marketing Techniques."

On the most basic level, you must market to your fans by presenting new music to them, letting them know it's available, and allowing word-of-mouth (the oldest of marketing techniques) to do its thing. Although this might sound simplistic, it underscores a very important point—namely, that you must continually be writing and producing new music, no matter what. The downside to social marketing techniques is the time that it can easily consume. Remember to maintain a healthy balance between creating music and creating fans. Without the former, you won't have any reason to do the latter.

Expanding Your Fan Base

As with many other topics in this book, there is a traditional way and a new way of expanding your fan base. The new way—which will probably come as no surprise—involves using social media marketing to increase your fans. The most straightforward example is the way Facebook users can ask others to be their fan or to "like" them. (More about this in Chapter 6.)

The traditional way can be summed up in one word: *touring*. If you prefer two words, those would be *playing live*.

It's funny how things come full circle sometimes. In the earlier days of rock 'n roll music, playing live and touring was a natural part of the marketing mix. This was how bands exposed new audiences to their music, promoted their albums, and increased their income. Then, somewhere along the line—even before the digital revolution—touring became too expensive and was reserved for only the top-tier acts that had their tours subsidized by large record companies (who would recoup those costs later from the artist).

The digital project studios added to this trend by allowing artists to produce albums in a spare bedroom of their house, using digital audio workstations and inexpensive duplicating facilities that could crank out thousands of CDs for pennies each. Why go out on the road? Why go out at all, for that matter? Everyone went into their individual bedrooms and fed themselves intravenously while cranking out new material. (Okay, I exaggerate to make a point.) Recordings became more polished and slick—so much so that it would be difficult for many independent acts to duplicate their recordings in a live venue without a lot of difficulty.

Figure 4.3 This image portrays a live, touring band. Actually, it's a shameless, opportunistic plug for my other book (but at least the cover is relevant here).

Now come full circle to the present. There are so many artists struggling to rise above the general noise level of thousands of other artists eager to make it in the music business that cranking out recordings isn't enough. This is where the rubber meets the road, as accomplished musicians can take advantage of playing live and demonstrate to audiences that they are the "real thing." And playing live in a variety of venues naturally means playing to new audiences and potentially expanding your fan base.

That's the good news. Now the bad news: This process takes time, lots and lots of time. You cannot go out on the road a couple of times and have thousands of fans as a result. So, you have to think in a different timeframe—not weeks, not months, but years. It can take four to five years to build a respectable following by playing live. This, of course, would be prohibitively

Figure 4.4 Father Time keeps rolling along. You may have to reset your expectations of how much time it takes to build a sizeable fan base.

expensive. So, your touring has to be part of an overall strategy—when to tour, where to tour, and how this corresponds to other things you are doing in your overall marketing mix. It can be done, and no one said it was going to be easy. The details of how to play live and tour effectively go beyond the scope of this particular book, but there are many other books and resources on the Internet to help you with this endeavor. One such book is *The Tour Book: How to Get Your Music on the Road* (Course Technology PTR, 2012).

What we *can* talk about in this book is how to leverage both traditional and social media marketing techniques to advance your career. This is what I'll cover next in Chapters 5 and 6, respectively.

5 Marketing Your Music the Traditional Way

The effects of the Internet and digital media on our lives have been so profound that it's difficult to summarize them in a sentence, a paragraph, or a book. That's partly because we are in the eye of this storm of change. The Internet has changed the way we communicate, the way we create, the way we educate, and the way we entertain. One thing is certain—the Internet has forever changed the music business, from the creative process to the way we market new music to others.

This chapter focuses on traditional marketing techniques. There are some who not only believe the newer social marketing (which includes leveraging sites such as MySpace, Facebook, Twitter, and a whole lot more) is the wave of the future, but who also simultaneously relegate traditional marketing to the distant past. And there are others, including me, who believe that a combination of traditional and social marketing is the best formula for success.

One thing I've learned over the years is that it's tempting to throw the proverbial baby out with the bathwater. I was working for Microsoft when CD-ROMs first debuted and everyone hailed the end of printed books. Obviously, that didn't happen, and the two media have coexisted for many years, each having its own distinct advantages. The threat of the end of printed books looms larger with the popularity of e-readers and the bankruptcies of brick-and-mortar outlets, such as Borders, Inc. Still, millions of people prefer the smell of paper and the thrill of browsing a real-life bookstore to downloading and reading a book on an electronic device.

Now, if someone were really brilliant back in the day, he would have known that CD-ROMs weren't the threat—the Internet and portable devices were the threats. Of course, that was a long time ago, and no one could see it coming. Likewise, we can't be certain what the marketing process will really look like 20 years from now. And so, because I believe in a combination of traditional and social marketing, I offer you information on both methods in this and the next chapters, and I show you how they can be used together.

If You Post It, Will They Come?

The answer, in a word, is no—not necessarily. (Yes, I know, that's three words.) The saying has many variations based on the original—"If you *build* it, will they come?" The "it" might refer to any type of product, from software to computer hardware to a new type of toaster. The phrase is often heard in the halls of marketing departments where product managers and product developers are in heated debates about the chances of their products' success. The old school of thought states that if a product is good enough, people obviously will buy it. The newer school states that unless some significant marketing energy is put behind a product (or service, for that matter), the chances of success are very limited, no matter how good the product actually is.

I suggest that marketing effort is not a luxury but a necessity in the music business, and that certainly applies to independent musicians getting their music heard.

This Just In: Good News/Bad News

The good news is that the Internet has changed all the rules. Now, instead of a few select artists being lucky enough to have a record contract, the playing field is wide open. With the Internet, it is now possible for one act to be marketed to millions of people, record label not required. Sure, small independent labels may be effective in this new arena (and there are the few superstars who will always be on the big labels), but the days of major corporations being a necessary part of the record-making machine seem to be pretty much over.

The bad news is everything I just wrote in the preceding paragraph. Because the playing field is wide open, the Internet is flooded with acts of all kinds and all levels of experience vying for the attention of those millions of prospective listeners. Maybe it's true that major labels are a thing of the past, but those same labels acted as a filter of sorts so that *some* level of quality and professionalism was present in the artists who made it to the surface. The often-used distribution models of one-to-many or many-to-one can be applied to the way music industry distribution has changed over the years, as shown in Figure 5.1. The old record industry allowed a few artists to reach many people. The current digital music industry has an overabundance of artists, but they're able to reach only smaller portions of the audience. The ideal of the future would be many artists having the ability to reach many people.

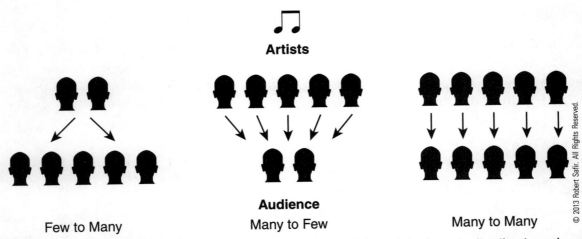

Figure 5.1 From left to right, the first diagram represents the old model of music distribution, the second is current digital music distribution, and on the right is the hopeful future.

All of this is to say that marketing now plays a more significant role—not that it didn't have an important role before—but perhaps now, more than ever, a *strategic* marketing mix has become a necessity, especially in light of new marketing methods.

Understanding the Marketing Mix

The marketing mix has traditionally consisted of the "four Ps"—product (or service), place, price, and promotion. Simply stated, it means putting out the right product at the right time and place and at the right price point. These four Ps correspond to the formal definition of the marketing mix (see Figure 5.2).

Figure 5.2 A classic definition of the marketing mix describes marketing strategy in terms of the four Ps.

There are other definitions of the marketing mix as well. From a tactical point of view, it can be considered as a combination of different marketing methods and techniques. It can be your marketing communications strategy, directing your message to your prospective customer (or fan) from all sides. Some have called this approach 360-degree marketing, although you can find dozens of other versions of what 360-degree marketing is supposed to mean. Figure 5.3 represents just one of them.

Figure 5.3 This is one of the models of the term "360-degree marketing," combining different marketing techniques to reach your target audience.

For the purposes of this book, I'm going to look at the marketing mix through a contemporary lens. I will view traditional marketing as all of the "old school" marketing methods, from positioning to PR to promotion. Social marketing will include such phenomena as MySpace, Facebook, Twitter, blogs, forums, and the like.

Somewhere between traditional and social marketing there was the practice of viral marketing or guerilla marketing, mostly utilizing websites and email as marketing tools. This was *before* social marketing and serves as a good example of a transition period between the old and the new marketing methods. These concepts are illustrated in Figure 5.4.

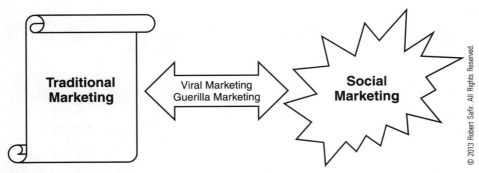

Figure 5.4 An illustration of traditional marketing, social marketing, and the transition that occurred between the two.

Now, take a look at traditional marketing and social marketing and see whether it doesn't make sense to create a formula for an even newer marketing mix. This mix might consist of a combination of traditional marketing, viral marketing, email marketing, social network marketing, and more—but likely will involve some of each.

A discussion of the fine details of every marketing tactic you can use, whether traditional, social, or a mix of both, is beyond the scope of this book. At a higher level is the need to have an understanding of marketing concepts. Once you understand those, you can determine which ones apply to you and then use your creativity to create a marketing plan of your own.

Understanding Traditional Marketing

Traditional marketing is the marketing we and our parents and their parents grew up with. According to the American Marketing Association, it is "the process for creating, communicating, delivering, and exchanging offerings that have value for customers, clients, partners, and society at large." If that sounds a bit corporate, that's because it is. Several of the processes that make up traditional marketing might apply to large businesses and corporations, while others have validity for us, the makers of music.

Traditional marketing in a company usually includes activities such as mission-statement development, positioning, market segmentation, value proposition, branding, public relations or publicity, promotion, and advertising. Sounds like this is the corporate stuff, right? Well, not necessarily—not when you understand how these things may apply on an individual level.

The Mission Statement

A mission statement accurately describes why a company or organization exists and what it hopes to accomplish in the future. It's a description of the organization's purpose—its reason for being. Mission statements can sometimes be a mouthful because marketers want to make sure that everything about the company is summarized in one paragraph. Sometimes the statement is full of jargon, but here's an example of a simple one from the Coca-Cola Company:

> *The Coca-Cola Promise: The Coca-Cola Company exists to benefit and refresh everyone it touches. The basic proposition of our business is simple, solid, and timeless. When we bring refreshment, value, joy and fun to our stakeholders, then we successfully nurture and protect our brands, particularly Coca-Cola. That is the key to fulfilling our ultimate obligation to provide consistently attractive returns to the owners of our business.*

Sometimes a company's mission statement is summarized in one line. For example, the mission statement for Starbucks is "To inspire and nurture the human spirit—one person, one cup, and one neighborhood at a time."

Now, how does a mission statement apply to you? On an individual level, your mission statement might be as follows: "My mission is to grow personally, professionally, and emotionally by using my unique perspective and my belief in others' inherent goodness and integrity." Sounds simple, but to do this daily and on a consistent basis might be difficult. That's what mission statements are for—they remind us why we do what we do so that we stay focused on the main objective.

An artist can have a mission statement. A band can have a mission statement—perhaps something like this:

> *"Our mission is to provide lifelong entertainment experiences for our community, country, and planet, through the performance of original music and live concerts. In the course of achieving our goals, we will be an example of good teamwork and friendship, resolving any internal disputes or obstacles that might get in our way. While competing at the highest level in the entertainment industry, we will provide opportunities for others to share our experience, whether they are fans or a part of our extended team."*

A business or enterprise usually publishes its mission statement in its marketing literature and on its website. You, as an artist or a band, do not have to publish a mission statement. But its true value is that it can keep you focused on your goal, remind you of why you do what you do, and increase your chances of success. You don't have to publish it to the world, but you can certainly integrate it into your thinking.

Positioning

Positioning is the process by which you create an image or perception in the mind of your customer. It often includes competitive positioning—how your product or service is better than the competition. When I was involved with marketing high-tech products for companies such as Microsoft, Digidesign, and Cisco Systems, the subject of positioning came up almost on a daily basis. Al Ries, sometimes co-writing with Jack Trout, wrote an excellent series of books on marketing, one of them called *Positioning: The Battle for Your Mind* (Warner Books, 1993). Another personal favorite of mine by these two authors was (and is) *The 22 Immutable Laws of*

Marketing (Harper Business, 1993). If you want only one book on traditional marketing techniques, *The 22 Immutable Laws of Marketing* is your best bet.

When you position a product, you define the competitive landscape in which you will compete, collect a sampling from existing customers on their perceptions of similar products in that "space," estimate the mindshare that the competitive products currently have (and how they are positioning in that space), and finally position your product.

Your product is you or your band. Using positioning, your goal is to establish a perception of your artistry in your target market—namely, the minds of your fans. To understand who your fans are and what makes them tick, you can use a process called *market segmentation*.

Market Segmentation

The process of market segmentation enables you to focus on the precise category of prospective customers (read: fans) that is most likely to purchase your offering. For large companies, this might mean dividing up the target market by size, age, sex, business function, and job responsibility. Once these qualities are defined within the target market, it's easier to zero in on the prospective customers' needs.

Perhaps the needs of your customer (music fans) are fairly straightforward—music may satisfy an emotional need that simply enhances their pleasure. The audience for music—that is, the mass market—is huge. With target marketing, you define your specific market's needs without trying to be all things to all people. What satisfies one customer—perhaps heavy metal music—might be completely inappropriate for another who likes smooth jazz. And the heavy metal music category (and most categories) can be further broken down into many subcategories.

Your job is to know where you fall in the scheme of things and what kind of characteristics you will find in your prospective customers or fans. A lot of this occurs naturally (without requiring a lot of market research) because the qualities of your act—your music, your appearance, your message—all appeal to a specific audience in the first place. You reach your audience because you are putting forth your particular brand. If you or someone in your band is more of the analytical type, then doing some exercises in market segmentation may be worthwhile.

Branding

Your exercises in positioning and market segmentation contribute to your understanding of your brand. Your brand is your identity—how you want your fans to perceive you. The degree of your success will make your brand range from unknown to a "brand name." Naturally, everyone wants to become a brand name, a name so recognizable that no explanation is necessary to understand what that brand name represents. Examples of this are Kleenex, FedEx, Amazon, Google, and the Beatles. You may not be the next Beatles, but you will want to get as high as possible on the branding ladder.

A brand might be a combination of characteristics—some of them innate, such as your body's physical appearance, and some of them created, such as how you clothe that body. Often a brand has components that are intangible. And more than likely, a brand is greater than the sum of its (tangible and intangible) parts.

Have you ever seen a commercial that has absolutely nothing to do with the actual product or company? The brand is so successful that it represents a larger feeling. The brand message can even be communicated without showing the product at all. Think Nike or Apple. There are some brands that are so strong that their (perceived) importance is much, much larger than the actual product, service, or company.

There may be more than you think when it comes to understanding the branding process, including concepts such as brand recognition, brand equity, brand franchise, and brand extension, to name a few. You can certainly succeed without this knowledge, but in a very competitive marketplace, the more you know, the better.

Value Proposition

The value proposition is one of the most corporate-sounding terms in marketing, and you may have a harder time relating to this term than to some of the others. Simply put, the *value proposition* is the statement of the sum total of benefits that your customers get for their money and/or time.

By the widest definition, you are likely to say that you provide customers with excellent entertainment. But other definitions are possible. Perhaps your band is active politically, so you provide political awareness. Perhaps your music makes people relax or brings people together in a social network. Knowing your value proposition is directly related to your positioning and, further, can make you stand out against your competition.

But most artists, let alone people in general, rarely think about this. Perhaps many people have internalized some form of a value proposition a long time ago and feel they don't need to revisit it. However, revisiting it from time to time can ensure that it reflects your value proposition as it stands today and, at the very least, brings your value proposition back into your consciousness.

One of the best ways to zero in on your specific value proposition is to see yourself from the outside. Pretend to be a potential fan at a concert looking up at the band on the stage and try to imagine how they see you and why you stand out from other artists. If you can define your value proposition, you can broadcast that message—overtly or subconsciously—to your ever-increasing audience.

The Three Ps—Public Relations, Publicity, and Promotion

PR is the "spin machine." PR is public relations and is the term most often used in the business or corporate world. Publicity is similar to PR, but it is the more common term in the entertainment business. Promotion is, well, promotion. Promotion activities are typically things such as tradeshows, endorsements, sponsorships, and direct mail.

While promotion may sometimes involve cash outlay, many PR activities are the type that can be executed for little or no money. If a magazine publishes a story about you as an artist, that's PR. The type of visibility that a magazine article can give you is arguably much better than if you were to take out a full-page ad in the same magazine. Indeed, this is an argument often made in debates regarding marketing budgets. Advertising is very expensive, so when budgets are tight, marketing managers (especially the ones higher up on the corporate ladder) prefer getting some free publicity to paying for full-page, four-color ads.

Some types of PR are more believable than others. One example is sponsorships. If Taylor Guitars sponsors you as an artist, people will probably think you must be a very talented performer. If they name a guitar after you and your name happens to be Taylor Swift, you probably don't need the extra publicity, but it certainly doesn't hurt! Take a look at the Taylor Guitars homepage in Figure 5.5.

The most elementary form of PR is the press release. You have probably seen press releases before, and they all follow a specific format (as indicated in the upcoming sidebar). A press release is written in third person, as if you were a reporter writing about the subject of the release. In other words, you would never say, "I released my new album today." Instead, you would write, "Peter Piper released his new album today."

When sending out a press release, the first thing to ask yourself is whether you really have some news. There's little worse than a press release that has nothing important to say. There should be

Figure 5.5 You're doing well if you are sponsored by a company such as Taylor Guitars. It's even sweeter if one of their guitar lines has your namesake on it.

some sort of story, whether it's simple, such as your new album release, or more complex, such as your new music licensing website that serves the film, television, and Internet industries.

Typical Press Release Format

FOR IMMEDIATE RELEASE

This usually appears on the upper-left side of the press release and is the first indicator that this is an "official" press release.

Headline

This is one major headline (occasionally accompanied by a secondary sub-headline) similar to what you see in newspapers. The headline is designed to attract attention, but it should be as factual as possible, or it won't be believable.

City, State, Month, Day, Year

These are the first items in the first paragraph. The text of the press release immediately follows *on the same line*.

Main Body

This is the text of the press release in paragraph form. The first sentence summarizes the entire story and entices the reader to read more.

About (Company Information)

This is the description of the company (or individual) and what they do, and it's often reflective of the mission statement.

Contact Information

This information includes the contact person's name, company name if appropriate, phone, fax, email, physical address, and relevant website address.

End

It is common for a press release to end with either - End - or ###. It's the official end of the press release, and there will be no doubt about it.

The press release is a delicate balance between spin and fact; it's neither one nor the other, but a bit of both. If the press release is written as straight spin, it will come off as hype. If it is written as pure fact, it will come off as dull. You need just enough spin to make the announcement in the press release seem exciting, as well as enough facts to substantiate your claims.

You can distribute your press release to your contacts via email. Most professionals use a press release wire service, such as PR Newswire, Business Wire, or WebWire. These services do cost money, but they have a prepared list of important press contacts organized into very specific markets. You may want to research these services a bit more to see whether they are something you need.

Advertising

Advertising is a means of getting your message out to persuade people to do something, whether it means buying your latest album or thinking that you're the best artist to come along in a century. (Be careful of that last one—advertising gives you more leeway than PR, but you still have to have your feet planted somewhere on the ground.)

Traditional advertising has relied on traditional media, including print (magazines, newspapers), broadcast television, cable television, radio, and, of course, the Internet. Advertising has grown to include any conceivable form of delivery and can now be found anywhere, from cereal boxes to sides of buses to bathroom stalls. (I didn't want to include that last one, but it demonstrates that there is no limit to what advertisers will do.)

Advertising is not cheap. A small newspaper ad can cost one or two thousand dollars. A television ad in primetime can cost up to $200,000, and if the commercial is run during the Super Bowl—well, we won't go there. Because advertising is expensive, it is important to measure its effectiveness. Companies have achieved this through specific telephone numbers related to a promotion or by having consumers ask about a very specific promotion. The big word here is *metrics*—that is, applying some form of measurement to the results of your advertising campaign.

Advertising in an environment such as the music business has its challenges, and never before have those challenges been as extreme as today. Because the business is undergoing such radical change, mostly as a result of the digital age and the Internet, the old forms of advertising are not as effective as they used to be. It is difficult to have a successful ad campaign in a magazine if the magazine itself is struggling for survival.

Like traditional advertising, traditional marketing has one foot in the past and a few toes in the future. The future may have more promise through social marketing or, as I stated earlier, some combination of both. So, it's time to take a close-up look at social marketing.

6 Leveraging Social Marketing Techniques

Before I dive into the topic of social marketing, perhaps I should revisit the definition of social marketing itself. I suppose I could take the lazy route and say that social marketing is anything outside the realm of traditional marketing. But that would sound lazy—and terse, cryptic, and possibly even sarcastic—and in general, it would be a copout of some sort. That said, social marketing should really be called *social-media marketing*, because it is marketing that leverages social-media sites, blogs, RSS feeds, and anything that generally comes under the heading of Web 2.0 (and further numerations of the web).

Today's web is riddled with articles from a variety of sources—both traditional and "new"—that debate the pros and cons of social-media marketing.

I am sensing an unusual seesaw motion in which new social-media sites, from Facebook to Twitter, are initially perceived as hype until the noise level drops enough that they gain stability and acceptance. At around the same time, a new social-media site—Pinterest comes to mind—pops up and goes through a similar process, until the next site comes along and the process repeats itself. Naturally, the decision-makers in these companies have to do an excellent job (in a very competitive and turbulent environment) to establish any corporate longevity to speak of. But assuming they do so, the seesaw continues to go up and down—and up again.

You can probably find pundits who still poo-poo social-media marketing and a larger number who take it very seriously. After all, virtually every company advertisement in every possible media outlet shouts "Visit Our Facebook Page" (although that has now been replaced by "Like Us on Facebook"). And then there are those ever-growing company logos at the bottom of all advertisements—Facebook, Twitter, YouTube, RSS, and mobile logos for Apple and Android operating systems. Social-media marketing seems to be here to stay.

The Act of Blogging

One of the first incarnations of social media marketing occurred when there was no such term as "social media marketing." Blogs (a portmanteau of the words "web" and "log") originally were simple logs or diaries that an individual posted on the Internet. Soon, blogs also became a means of creating one's own editorial space by focusing on a particular topic and making regular entries, reporting an event or supporting an idea.

If a blog could be authored by an individual, why not have a blog authored by an individual from a particular company? Well, that's precisely what came next, with many executives, including company CEOs, writing their own blogs. The company blog accomplished several things. It allowed a company to get its message out. The blog provided a means of creating buzz. It also created a new way to gain insight into a company's customers—to find out what they *really* think about a brand or a product.

All of these benefits apply to individuals as well, including music makers. Bands can have blogs; artists can have blogs. A band's blog may have reports from its concert tour; an artist's blog may have updates on how the latest studio recording sessions are progressing. In short, a blog can have anything you want in it.

But the term "content is king," although overused, is still valid. Just because you *can* blog about something doesn't mean you *should* blog about it. Like other content, blog content needs to gain a reader's attention, have a story of some significance, and provide a reason for the reader to follow the blog.

What's the difference between a blog and a website? If you were to suppose a blog and a website had identical content, the difference would rely on the real-time experience of a blog. A blog is more immediate, timelier, and, generally speaking, more recent than a static website. A website needs to pull in readers. A blog pushes out its contents.

With all that in mind, it's also interesting to note that a blog can be a part of a website or a part of a MySpace page. Or it can live on its own as a blog hosted by a site specializing in blogs, such as WordPress or Blogger.com.

An individual may blog to keep in touch with friends and relatives. A company may blog to understand and influence its customers. An artist or band may blog to increase its fan base.

Blogging is good. I highly recommend it.

The Dawn (and Dusk) of MySpace

MySpace was known for a long time as *the* place to go for social networking. It became a huge destination for people of all types—at first, young people looking for other young people with a desire to make friends; then professionals from all walks of life who wanted to network, promote themselves, and make friends; and ultimately, everybody and anybody had a MySpace page.

Before MySpace, anyone who wanted to create her own individual website needed a degree from MIT and 10 years of computer programming experience. MySpace made it easy to have a "page." All you had to do was sign up.

It wasn't long until a prevalence of musicians, bands, artists, and singers seemed to dominate the MySpace population. You could sign up as an artist/musician and have your own space to upload your original music, play it, sell it, announce your touring schedule, create a blog, and in every way, shape, and form promote yourself 'til the cows came home. And perhaps most important of all, you could (and still can) upload 10 of your own original tracks for people to either listen to or download. In Figure 6.1, you can see my main MySpace page with the music player on the right.

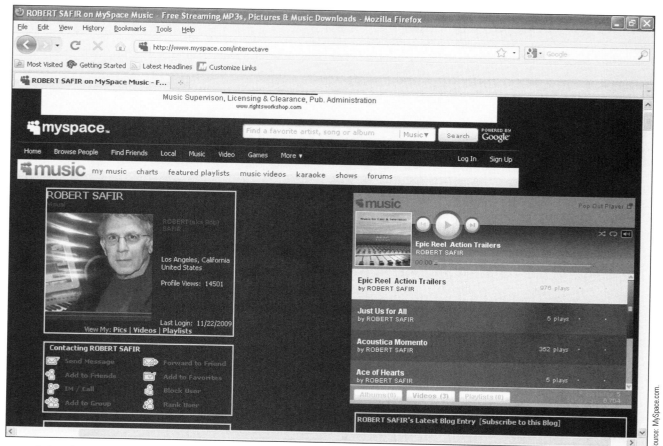

Figure 6.1   This is my MySpace page showing the music player on the right.

Source: MySpace.com.

The naysayers would always point out, however, that nobody ever came up through the ranks for real pop music visibility by having a MySpace page. That's no longer true, and one example among many is Kate Voegele, shown in Figure 6.2. She and other artists went from relative obscurity to high visibility by way of MySpace.

Figure 6.2 Kate Voegele, shown here on the MySpace Records page, is one of several successful independent artists who emerged from MySpace.com.

But what goes up must come down, as they say. Once the darling of online social sites, MySpace has lost favor and market share to others, such as Facebook. Once upon a time you *had* to have a MySpace page. Now you have to have a Facebook page.

The one exception to this might be MySpace Music. The management at MySpace realized that they could leverage their huge population of music makers and music lovers into nothing less than their own label, which they formed in 2005 as a joint venture with Interscope Records. Today, MySpace has positioned itself as a social networking site that specializes in or focuses on music, with its own label, MySpace Records. How successful it will be as a label remains to be seen, and recent events such as dismal earnings and the sale of the company altogether don't bode well for the future.

MySpace Records is the label. However, label aside, there is a Music page on MySpace at www.music.myspace.com, shown in Figure 6.3. The Music page includes Music Videos, Music Video Charts, News, Shows & Events, Playlists, Artist's Activity, and a whole lot more. Music playlists can be selected from categories such as Major, Indie, Unsigned, or Recently Added by Friends.

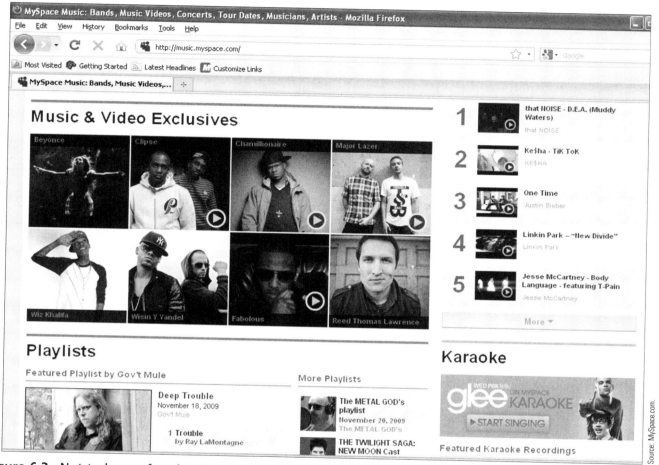

Figure 6.3 Not to be confused with MySpace Records, the record label, is the music page on MySpace, known, oddly enough, as MySpace Music.

There is also a Music Video page that features staff picks, hot videos, and recent videos (categorized by artists your friends are watching and artists you're watching). Figure 6.4 shows the MySpace Video page with a video of Beyoncé currently playing.

So, you might be wondering how you can be featured on MySpace.

Well, if you mean the label, MySpace Records, you would have been noticed by now and signed a contract with MySpace/Interscope. But as an artist, how do you get featured on the MySpace Music page? Unfortunately, it's not up to you. The answer is not unlike the method of climbing

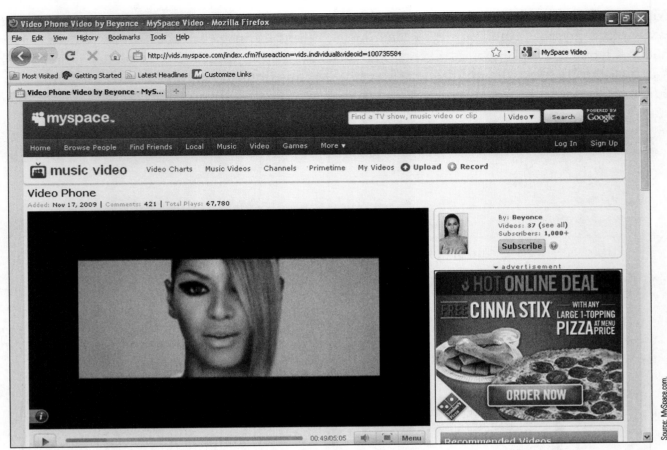

Figure 6.4 A specific channel for music videos is in the Video section on the MySpace site.

up the "charts" at YouTube—you have to have tons of traffic coming to your own MySpace page. Then you get noticed (by MySpace staff). If you have enough buzz about you or the band, you may hear from a MySpace staffer.

What MySpace Says about Becoming a Featured Artist on the MySpace Music Page How does MySpace choose featured artists, musicians, and comedians? We're totally committed to celebrating the best in music, art, and comedy. We get really excited when we discover new talent and get to showcase their work! Just so you know, we don't accept artist requests for feature coverage, since we prefer to leave it to the MySpace community to decide.

When we see a lot of traffic on an artist profile, we check it out. If there's a good buzz, we sometimes give them a shout out.

You need to build up enough traffic to your own page before you can become a featured artist or have a highly visible musical presence on MySpace. But in the meantime, you need to get your music on your main page and use every tool you can to build traffic. This means not only having your music (and your music videos, if you have any) easily accessible on your page (I've got my videos visible right on my main page, as shown in Figure 6.5), but also using every method you can to build awareness. The tasks are the ones I've been discussing—post your music and your music videos, create a blog, and "friend" people. (Yes, *friend* is a verb now, as is *unfriend*.) Post your touring schedule or appearances, get involved in groups, and use the bulletin board to make announcements that go out to your list of friends.

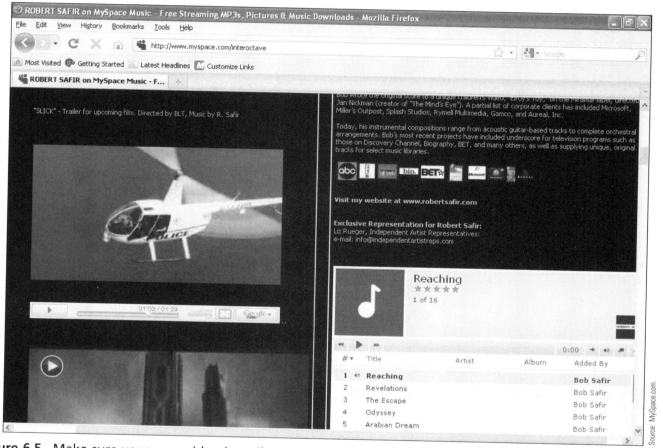

Figure 6.5   Make sure your own video is easily accessible on your main MySpace page, as illustrated here on my MySpace page.

Finally, network with (or friend) the type of people you would want to hang out with or get to know on a professional level. Those people could be your peers—other artists or bands. They might also be the managers, agents, or independent labels you would like to work with. But here's a word of caution: Don't throw yourself at your music business connections and plead with them to visit your page. Such behavior comes off as being desperate. It ignores the fact that these particular contacts also have a life, and probably a very busy one. Sure, you want them to visit your page. But use other methods, such as social skills (even if they are actually *online* social skills), to get people interested enough to hear your music.

One of the coolest features of MySpace is the Artist Dashboard. This Dashboard provides you with statistics on your page views; the total songs played; the songs played today; other song statistics, including trends; and the demographics of your audience. A summary of your Dashboard appears on the page in which you manage your profile, as shown in Figure 6.6. Clicking View All Stats in the lower-right corner brings you to the complete Dashboard page, shown in Figure 6.7.

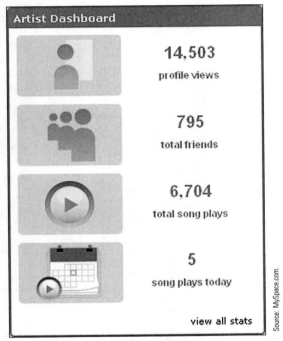

Figure 6.6 The summary of the Artist Dashboard appears when you manage your main page after signing in.

The Artist Dashboard comes complete with charts and graphs, and it's free. This is the equivalent of having an analyst (not a shrink, but a number cruncher) on your personal payroll. Use these statistics to understand who your audience is, what tracks they like, and what these numbers and charts show about trends relative to your music.

For MySpace to work for you, you must be involved and active with it. If you do that, you can increase your traffic. If you increase your traffic, you increase the likelihood that your music will be heard and that your career just might take off. What may be in doubt is whether MySpace has the same influence it did a few years ago. Time will tell.

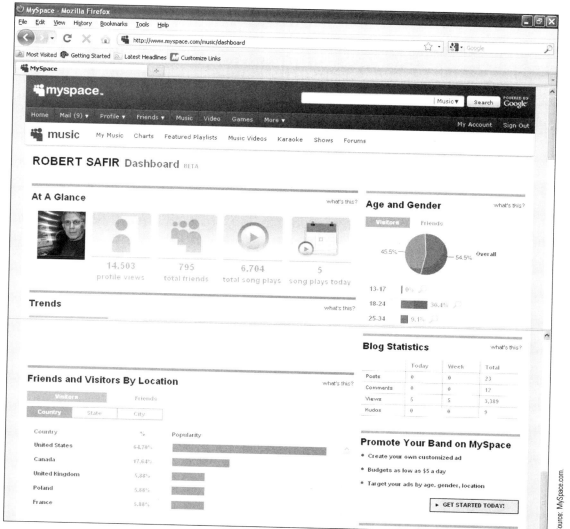

Figure 6.7 Clicking on View All Stats on the Artist Dashboard summary brings you to this page, loaded with statistics that can be useful in understanding your audience.

iLike imeem Ahh, for the love of acronyms, there has to be a joke in here, somewhere. But what is no joke is the rapidity with which the music landscape changes. As of this writing, the formerly independent and mostly alternative sites, iLike and imeem, were individual companies. But now they have been acquired by MySpace, and the actual names *iLike* and *imeem* are no longer in use. Between MySpace Music, iLike, and imeem, it's not yet clear what long-term strategy lives in the minds of MySpace music execs. Streaming, downloading, purchasing, subscribing, or any combination of these is certainly possible. What it means for the music business in general is more uncertain. Time will tell, and by the time you read this book, the music landscape might be quite different than it is now.

The Rise of Facebook

Facebook's rapid rise in popularity has led it to a position no one could have predicted in the early days of MySpace domination. Facebook is now the "Hertz Cars" of the social networking sites, while MySpace has become the "Avis" of the bunch. Translated into plain English, in case you haven't seen a lot of television commercials for Hertz or Avis, Facebook is now number one, whereas MySpace is number two and falling.

One of the main features of Facebook is the Wall, where you and your Facebook friends can post messages for others to see. You also can upload photos, share information via the News Feed, update your status, and gently poke a friend who usually pokes you in kind. You can join networks, form groups, and search for and add new friends to your heart's content. These are all features you can access and change via your Home page or Profile page. See my Profile page in Figure 6.8. (As you can see in the figure, Facebook pages tend to be text-oriented and not as graphical as some social sites.)

Figure 6.8 Here is my Profile page on Facebook.

Facebook also lets you upload videos. Your video is compressed and converted to a Flash file that plays right there on your Profile page. This is one way to put your music video out there, but it's not the only way.

What may be of more importance to you as an artist and music producer is the Facebook feature known as *Pages*. Pages allow Facebook members to become a fan of a product, a service, or an individual. (Herbie Hancock has a Page as a professional artist, shown in Figure 6.9.) You might think of a Facebook Page as a commercial version of a regular Facebook account. And speaking of commercial, if you have a Page, you are also able to advertise, using pay-per-click or pay-per-impression advertising rates. As an advertiser, you get access to real-time reporting and other statistical results related to your ad.

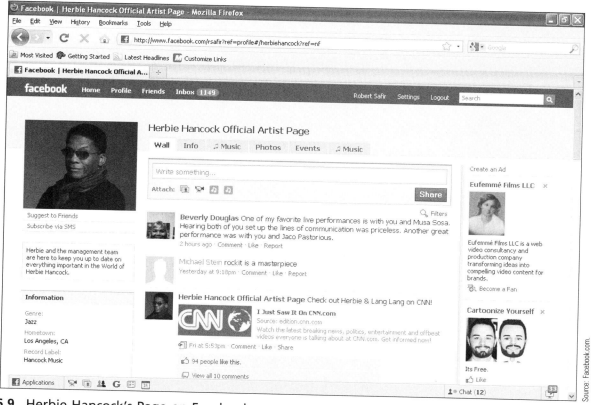

Figure 6.9 Herbie Hancock's Page on Facebook.

Online Advertising Rates   There is a lot to learn if you want to pursue online advertising (whether on Facebook, Google, or anywhere else). In brief, here are a couple of terms you ought to know:

- **PPC.** Pay-per-click: With this model, you pay only when your ad is clicked on.

- **CPC.** Cost-per-click is what you pay if there is "click-through," meaning when visitors click on an ad that results in them visiting your website.

- **Flat-rate and bid-based PPC.** Rates for PPC can be based on a fixed flat rate, or they can be bid on. You name the price, but the highest bidder's (meaning your competitors who are also price-bidding) results are displayed first.

- **CPM.** Cost-per-thousand, based on views (cost per thousand views). This is part of the pay-per-impression model.

The topic of online advertising covers huge territory. Click-through rate, cost-per-click, cost-per-impression, and conversation rate are just a few of the terms you'll discover if you pursue online advertising. Perhaps the best known of all online advertising concepts is Google AdWords, in which you choose keywords relative to your business. When users search on these keywords, your ad will come up next to Google's search results.

Although it is possible to upload videos to a regular Facebook account and to upload music-only tracks using several third-party apps available through Facebook, the Pages option allows more professional-looking results. You will find Pages from some of the music industry's most popular artists on Facebook Pages.

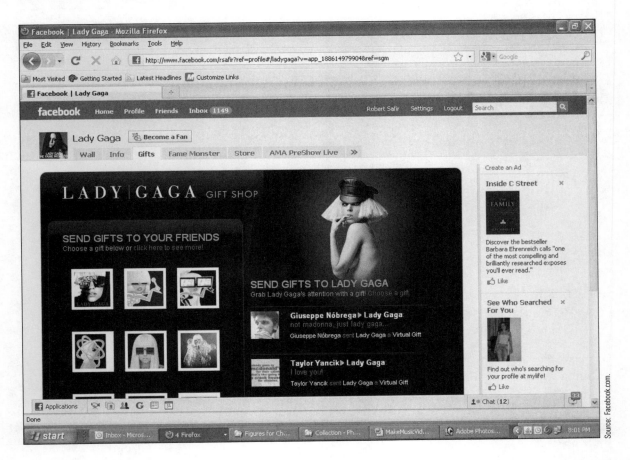

Using Facebook Pages does *not* require you to participate in online advertising. The basic concept of Pages and fans helps to spread your message virally. When a fan interacts with your Page, stories linking to your Page can be directed via News Feed to *their* friends. When these friends interact with your Page, the News Feed keeps spreading the word, via word-of-mouth, to a wider network of friends.

You can do many things on a Page that you cannot do on a regular Profile page. Figure 6.10 shows how you can browse or search for a specific artist. (You can see how the "King of Pop" appears at the very top of the list.) Figure 6.11 shows U2's Video section selected from its artist Page. A professional Page enables you to host numerous videos from a central location as opposed to scattered videos showing up on a Wall or News Feed on a "regular" page.

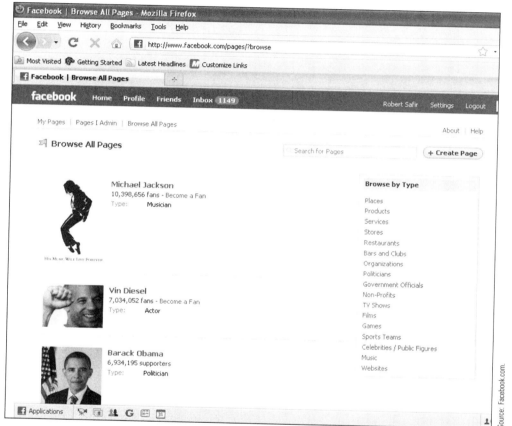

Figure 6.10 You can use Facebook's Browse and Search functions to locate a specific artist.

You also have the capability to send out messages to fans by clicking Send Update to Friends. This can be any kind of announcement, sales promotion, or news of an upcoming concert or event.

Facebook is in a very good position in the social marketing landscape. How all of the competition in this landscape plays out remains to be seen. From your perspective, as an artist and musician, you need to keep on top of the fast-moving developments that occur in social media marketing. There are always two fronts to keep track of: the social media sites available to the

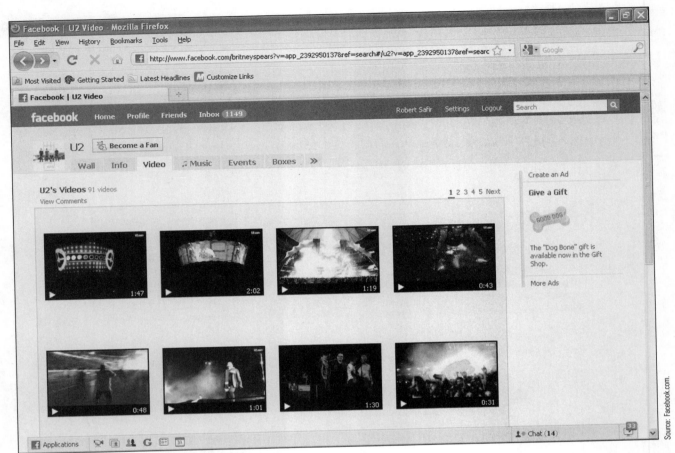

Figure 6.11 Shown here is U2's Video section from its artist page.

public and the sites (social or not) that are focused on the music business. Those are your playgrounds.

Don't Blink or You'll Miss the Latest Social-Media Changes During the course of writing this book, MySpace tanked in the popularity polls and users left in droves to hang out at Facebook. Sometime thereafter, MySpace announced that music star Justin Timberlake was coming onboard the company to breathe new life into MySpace Music. It was big news, but as of now, the long-term prognosis of this move is unknown.

In another vein, Facebook is notorious for making sweeping changes to their user interface, features, and policies (especially *privacy* policies). As of today, the well-known layout of Facebook has been altered in a big way, with the timeline taking precedence on your Facebook homepage. Now everything is organized by time, whether you want it be or not, and a large picture takes up most of the real estate on your homepage.

What is not known is how people will receive this change. Other changes in the past have nearly caused riots. Furthermore, it is questionable as to what effect this change will have for artists with their own page. (This would also be true for companies that have their own page and people who "like" them.)

I don't have the answers to these questions, but what can be uncomfortable for many is that perhaps no one has these answers—at least, not yet. So, if you're spending a lot of time and staking a lot of faith in creating sites as a vehicle to promote your music, be on the lookout. Don't blink, or you'll miss the latest social-media changes—and those changes can affect your marketing strategies.

And a last note about Facebook: When I began writing this book, Facebook was a private company, and by the time I completed the book, they held an IPO and became a public company. This is an important turning point, because on the plus side, it may become an even more important vehicle for you as a musician and songwriter. On the extreme minus side, if the stock price doesn't hold water and people sour on the entire Facebook idea, this could lead to another bubble that bursts someday. Time will tell.

Using Twitter and Tweets

The words "Twitter" and "Tweets" sound like something from a Warner Bros. cartoon, but they're no laughing matter. Twitter is a social marketing tool that enables you to send and receive short (up to 140 characters) messages known as *Tweets*. These messages can travel by a number of means, including the Twitter website, email, text messaging, and instant messaging. Tweets started out as simple updates on what you were doing at any given moment, such as "just combed hair, listening to Mariah C. on the 405 south." (Within this message are a couple of potential social problems—combing one's hair while driving is one of them, as is sending a text message while on the freeway. But that's another topic altogether.) There are a few *million* Tweets posted every day by more than a million users. Figure 6.12 shows just a few Tweets from a moment in time.

Although Tweets began life as simple messages about a person's status, it wasn't long before people realized that they could use Tweets for more commercial purposes, such as sharing information about their products or services. Short electronic messages of any kind are sometimes grouped under the heading of "microblogs" or status updates (which is also one of the features on MySpace or Facebook).

Twitter is no longer considered a simple, personal message service for the under-30 crowd. It has grown to be used in a vast number of ways, including the following:

- Promotion
- Advertising
- Surveys
- Emergencies

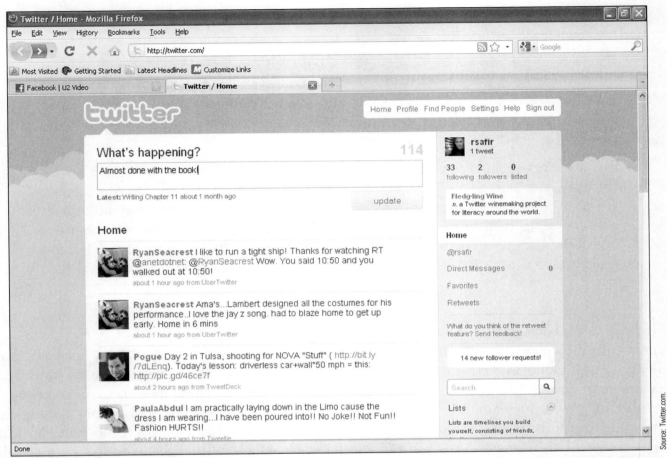

Figure 6.12 With Twitter, you can follow updates on what people are doing—and they can follow you as well.

- Political campaigns

- News

Twitter was even used as a communication platform during a Shuttle mission to service the Hubble Telescope. And more recently, Twitter (along with Facebook) was a means of communication that enabled uprisings in Egypt, Libya, Bahrain, and other countries in the Middle East. I'm not saying that the social networks *caused* the uprisings—I'm saying that they *enabled* them.

Many people question and debate the viability of Twitter for any purpose beyond casual conversation. Can Twitter really be used as a marketing tool? You can, in fact, use Tweets to:

- Send out updates on your band.

- Promote special offers, such as CDs on sale.

- Link to news pages (or for that matter, any page) on your own website.

- Create buzz.

- Reinforce your brand as an artist or band.

If you decide to use Twitter, make sure you get familiar with Twitter etiquette and the proper format for creating Tweets. In general, it's a good idea to keep the tone informal, conversational, and personal. This is not your father's advertising vehicle. Try to be less "in your face" and more "hey, check this out."

Visit Us, Follow Us, Join Us

The Internet has given you an easy way to spread your message, above and beyond a specific site in which you choose to participate. Now, in the form of buttons, badges, or plain old links, you can be an electronic Johnny Appleseed. You do this by placing these badges everywhere in which you have a presence, such as "Visit us on Facebook" (or MySpace or your YouTube Channel, and so on). You can see an example of these buttons in Figure 6.13.

It's the easiest, quickest form of cross-marketing ever developed. Use it wisely and frequently.

About LinkedIn

I wanted to briefly mention LinkedIn, which is more of a business-oriented social networking site. It allows you to establish a linked network of contacts or *connections*, which, through the laws of mathematics, continues over time to expand your network of additional contacts. You can use LinkedIn to make contact with people you wouldn't ordinarily be able to reach (in the

Figure 6.13 Everyone can find everyone else with badges or buttons. You can find them, visit them, and follow them. Just try not to annoy them.

boring, mundane physical world) and even to find or announce information on jobs or business opportunities.

LinkedIn also features groups. Anyone can form these groups, and almost anyone can join one, the main requirement being that you are actually a member of a certain community or discipline. There is a place in which you can provide answers to questions posed by other LinkedIn members, which is an opportunity to show your expertise in a particular subject. You can drive members to your own blog, and you can link to your own website.

LinkedIn may not be the ideal place for an up-and-coming band or artist, at least in terms of building a fan base. However, as a business-oriented site, you may find it useful in other ways, such as connecting with agents, managers, publicists, record labels, and so on. You will also find ways to connect to colleagues—other artists, songwriters, and musicians. Think of LinkedIn as a social network for the business aspects of your career and the other social sites I discussed as social marketing sites to connect you with and build up your fan base.

One interesting fact is that LinkedIn continues to grow at a rapid pace, and users are, in fact, finding ways to establish business connections that would have been otherwise impossible without the benefits of leveraging LinkedIn. Apparently many others agree, as LinkedIn went public with an IPO in May 2011 and raised boatloads of cash.

And speaking of IPOs, Facebook went public on May 18, 2012, but not without lots of problems. There were computer glitches on NASDAQ during the first several hours of trading, causing millions of dollars in misplaced trades. Today's stock price is only $17 and change, less than half the value of the initial $38 offering, which only lends credence to the claim that Morgan Stanley's opening price was way too high. Now there are many lawsuits involving Facebook, Morgan Stanley, NASDAQ, Yahoo, stockholders—the list goes on. How refreshing to know that Facebook is a company that is officially "all growed up."

Using Other Marketing Methods

You can view a variety of marketing methods as a part of both traditional and social media. They are as follows (in no particular order):

- **Email blasts.** Sending emails to a list has origins in the corporate world. You can use email blasts to promote events to your fans or news to the music industry. I just advise you not to overdo this method and to give people an opportunity to opt out of receiving your messages.

- **Links to and from other sites.** You may find sites where you'd like to have some sort of presence. Perhaps the site would be interested in having a presence on your website. Trading links is the way to accomplish this—you do so by identifying the best contact on the site you're interested in and suggesting cross-linking. If it becomes a done deal, the links can be in the form of a URL or a button, a banner, or even a photo or video.

- **Trading banner ads.** As in the preceding case, an appropriate or relevant trade of banner ads might be a possibility. It's a lot cheaper than having to purchase a banner ad. Keep in mind, though, that the once-glorious world of banner advertising is not as attractive or welcomed as it once was.

- **Optimized search.** Learn what you need to do to include important keywords about you or your band so that you will come up often in search engine results. There is both a science and an art to this, and search engine optimization (SEO) is the subject of many books and articles.

- **Landing pages.** These are pages that you specifically build on your own website, usually to measure the results of a particular marketing campaign. Say, for example, that you are giving away free T-shirts to the first 25 fans who respond to a contest question. The question may be located on your home page or anywhere on the Internet. The thing to do is to have respondents go to a specific URL or landing page on your site where you can measure the number of actual respondents to this promotion.

- **Contests, promotions, giveaways.** These are fairly self-explanatory. But as with landing pages, make sure you have a way to measure results. Otherwise, you won't really know where to put your time and energy to promote yourself.

- **Web analytics.** Measuring traffic on your landing page is one thing, but analyzing traffic on your site—from where people enter the site to what pages they usually migrate to—can tell you a lot about the overall effectiveness of your web design. Google provides some free tools for this, and several software companies make applications specifically designed for this purpose.

- **Internet forums.** Participating in Internet forums is another way to have a presence and to get additional insight into what other people (including fans) are thinking. You can have a forum of your own making as well as participate in relevant forums that already exist.

And the Winner Is...

In the previous two chapters, I discussed two different schools of thought—traditional marketing and social marketing—noting that there are ardent believers on each end of the spectrum. Today, there is no shortage of blogs on which one is better than the other.

Many people refer to social marketing as *relationship marketing*. Perhaps social marketing, with an emphasis on relationships, has been the missing ingredient in traditional marketing. Or, just to make your head buzz, maybe it is traditional marketing that has been missing from social marketing. People will continue to debate the effectiveness of traditional marketing and social media marketing. As I have stated, I believe a blend of both approaches works best. Your mileage may vary, but keep an open mind when you begin your marketing efforts and see where that takes you. Usually surprises are in store.

Finding a Formula for Foolproof Marketing

If you'd like a foolproof method of marketing your music on the Internet, you may have to look elsewhere—and you may have to look for a long, long time. None of the methods discussed here is a guarantee of anything. Nor is there an absolute formula for which marketing methods, and in what combination, you should use. A lot of it comes from trial and error. But if your experimentation is built on some basic knowledge of marketing techniques—old school and new school—your chances of success are greatly increased.

Note   There's plenty more to learn about social-media marketing. See Chapter 10, "Latest Trends in Digital Music," for more detailed information on social-media marketing trends, techniques, and strategies.

---

7 Music and Merchandising

What is merchandising? In the broadest definition, merchandising is any practice that contributes to the sale of a product to a consumer. Where merchandising is seen in the most tangible form is at the retail level. Here, products are displayed in such a way as to stimulate and entice customers to make a purchase. This is where you see the utmost in product design, packaging, and visual displays to maximize sales.

You can look to the movies to see merchandising in one of its major forms, as superheroes and spaceships are turned into toys that line retail shelves. Merchandising is often tied to calendar events, such as back-to-school sales that appear, well, just before school starts.

There is another definition of merchandising that describes it as a marketing practice in which the brand or image from one product is used to sell another. In this sense, your logo or photograph on a coffee mug is used to sell another product—*you*.

Often there is a merchandiser who purchases a product from a manufacturer and sells it to the consumer, using an array of tools from his merchandising toolkit. But, as you already know, *you* must wear many hats, including the one that says "Merchandiser" on the front.

Encore: Remember the Target Audience

Merchandising is not done in a vacuum. Nor is merchandising done as a last-minute exercise. Professionals spend many months planning, organizing, and executing their merchandising strategy and tactics.

Companies large and small conduct focus groups, testing their product and merchandising plans. They determine what colors to use, what buzzwords to use, and how the signage should look in a store.

You may not have the time or resources to conduct focus groups—and in fact, focus groups are not as relevant to an upcoming artist or band. Your focus groups are the first audiences you played for. This is where you tested out your music. Over time, you were able to get a sense of who your audience was and what they liked. This, in a sense, was your focus group.

The fine tuning of this exercise in identifying your audience was discussed in Chapter 4, "Knowing Your Audience." The concepts of positioning, market segmentation, and branding are a few of the tools that help define and target your audience. These are the things to keep in mind when you carry out a merchandising plan. Everything you do in merchandising should be consistent with the concepts you defined in your marketing plan.

Why Merchandising Matters

Well, the truth is, merchandising won't matter *that* much to you if you're signed to a major label. The resources they have include their own merchandising departments—or at the very least, one of those companies they can contract with to execute merchandising on behalf of the label and artist. Sure, the artist would have *some* input, depending on how much clout she has. But the major activities of planning, developing, and carrying out a merchandising campaign would be up to the hired guns.

So, just like many other parts of the marketing mix that do-it-yourselfers have to worry about, merchandising is an integral part of *your department.*

There are many reasons why merchandising is important to you, but to keep things simple, I will discuss three of the biggest ones.

Reason Number One: Survival

Just in case you've forgotten the gist of the previous six chapters, I will remind you that you're in an extremely competitive business—with many unsigned artists becoming road kill along the way to "making it big." That's why you're looking into books like this one or going to seminars with similar topics. You're trying to use every trick in the book to elevate your visibility in an over-crowded market. Yes, we all know how talented you are. But I have already said that talent is a given. If you don't have talent, you're not even in the game to begin with.

And so, my talented friends, you can look at merchandising as another tool that might ultimately help you pay the rent—or at least be an ongoing part of the business you love.

Reason Number Two: Promotion

Okay, I'll assume you're surviving and that you're still with us. What good is merchandising now?

I mentioned at the beginning of this chapter that another definition of merchandising describes it as a marketing practice in which the brand or image from one product is used to sell another. This is how you need to look at it. There may be times when you ask yourself: Why in the world am I sitting here worrying about the look of our coffee mug? Or our T-shirt? Remember, you're selling—or promoting—your band or yourself as an artist.

Reason Number Three: Your Fans

Your fans need you. They need to feel close to you. They are thrilled when they can identify themselves with your music or your act. But you are not going to be able to reach out and touch everyone, nor will they all fit backstage after your performance. Your fans want to take a piece of you with them. And this is a very good thing, because you will have all sorts of merchandise that you can offer them.

As I mentioned in Chapter 6, the marketing of today can be looked at as *relationship marketing*. And relationships are a two-way street. Gone are the days when there was a huge chasm between you and your fans. All of your blogging, Tweeting, and Facebook activity is a way to create, build, and foster a relationship with your fans. Merchandising is the physical manifestation or means of maintaining that relationship. Perhaps there is a fan or two that uses your band's coffee mug as a transitional object after your concert is over and they've gone home. *Perhaps*—however, this is a topic of another book, possibly a book that a psychologist or sociologist might write.

Try to think of these concepts when you go about the business of creating your merchandise. You can look at merchandising as a necessary and trivial task. But you would be better off thinking of it as a tool that establishes two-way communication with your fans and comes complete with an emotional impact that can last long after you've left on your bus tour of the USA.

8 The Aesthetics of Developing Merchandise

Like a lot of other creative arts, developing the right look for your merchandise is a combination of both science and art. Think of the science as the marketing principles that I have discussed throughout the book. Think of the art as, well, art—but with a twist. The art has to be an expression of *you*. Not all art is the same, and not all musicians are the same. So how do you go about creating the right art—and thus the right merchandise that is a reflection of you?

Establishing a Look and Feel for Merchandise

You may have heard the expression "look and feel" when it comes to the aesthetics of a website or software program. Look and feel are the graphics elements that best represent a subject, whether it be a company, a product, a band—or you. Just as your music has an audio identity, your artistry has a visual identity. What do you look like? What colors? What messages are conveyed by your look and feel?

It's easy to understand look and feel simply by taking a tour of the history of album covers. Today, the same thing can be accomplished by a tour of artists' websites.

By now, you can probably surmise that there is a thread running through everything in this book. To market yourself, you have to position yourself. To position yourself, you have to segment your target audience—as well as gain an understanding of your competition. You have to know what genre you belong to. When you do these things (as well as the extended list of other marketing tasks), they help establish your brand. Your brand is an extension of your identity. Your identity is conveyed by your look and feel and, ultimately, your merchandise.

You can see why a keen understanding of your own marketing mix is a precursor to anything you do in your area of the music business.

If you don't believe me, ask Lady Gaga.

Choosing the Right Colors

Because this book is printed in black and white, I strongly encourage you to look up examples on the web or in print so that you can fully understand the following concepts.

A Brief History of Color Theory

Cool colors and warm colors each convey different meanings. Cool colors can express calmness or coolness or even coldness. Warm colors, naturally, express warmth or excitement, whereas neutral colors can tone down colors of either extreme. And there you have it—a full understanding of color theory in three sentences!

Check out color theory by Googling it on the web. A very basic explanation can be found at desktoppub.about.com/od/choosingcolors/p/color_meanings.htm, but there are mountains of websites on this topic available for you to study.

Continuing on, you might want to check out en.wikipedia.org/wiki/Color_theory.

Wikipedia goes into more detail, including another concept you might remember from your early school days—complementary colors.

Appoint the Right Person for the Gig

I should point out that if you, the reader, do not have natural instincts (or desire) to get into the nitty gritty of color theory—or for that matter, graphics in general—then you should appoint someone in your band (or your roadie, or your girlfriend/boyfriend, or whoever might have the talent) to take on these tasks. As a musician, you understand that some talents are innate, and others can be learned and developed—depending on the amount of time and energy you have to put into it.

Creating Your Logo

The first order of business is defining the term "logo" and understanding how having one applies (or doesn't apply) to you. So let's start with the definition.

> Logo: Noun: A symbol or other small design adopted by an organization to identify its products, uniform, vehicles, etc., to aid and promote instant public recognition.

Logos may be purely graphic (such as symbols or icons), or they may be composed of the name of the company or organization.

One very recognizable logo that is simply a mark or symbol is that of Nike. You certainly must have seen and recognized Nike's logo at some time. Another symbol that you might recognize is Apple's logo.

McDonald's logo has the famous golden arches and includes the company name. After decades of using this, McDonald's is demonstrating how a logo can be "reinvented" by either eliminating the logo altogether or replacing the company name with a tagline, "I'm Lovin' It." These kinds of variations can work, but only once your company (or you) is so famous that your logo doesn't require the name.

Companies go to great extremes to protect their intellectual property through trademarks, which can include company names, logos, and other graphic elements. As of this writing, there is an interesting controversy going on with Apple's name for their online store that sells applications or "apps," called the App Store. When Amazon.com named their store the App Store, Apple threatened a lawsuit. Amazon and other companies argued that you cannot trademark something as generic as an "App Store." Apple countered with the argument that you cannot trademark something as generic as "Windows." Amazon's website for apps is currently named "Appstore" (one word). As of now, it's too soon to say whether this difference is enough to settle the argument.

So, how does the concept of logos apply to the music business? Although there may not be as many music logos as there are company logos, consider the logos for a few famous bands.

Source: Metallica™, the Beatles™, the Rolling Stones™.

You can see how powerful these images are. Now, you might argue that you're not in the same league as these groups and that a logo is superfluous at this point in your career—and that's a justifiable opinion. A logo is not an absolute necessity. However, if your name—or your band's name—lends itself to a graphic treatment in the form of a logo, there is no reason not to create one. Having your brand or identity encapsulated in one streamlined graphic image is a major accomplishment. A logo can add believability and authority to your act, and if you do become rich and famous, you just might have something that adds brand equity to your name. And last but not least, a logo lends itself very well to the topic at hand—merchandise.

Using the Tools of the Trade

When it comes to graphics, there are many tools you can use to create visual magic. Just as the computer on your desktop is more powerful than the computer that took the Apollo astronauts to the moon, the computing power on your desktop can provide you with more power than type-setters and artists had available to them just two decades ago.

Adobe Products

Adobe Photoshop is the essential application for creating your graphics. It is available on both Mac and PC platforms and is the standard application in use today for graphics. If you are even an intermediate-level user of Photoshop, you can go a long way in shaping the look of your band's logo, album art, and lots of merchandise.

If you find Photoshop too daunting—and some people do—then definitely consider getting Adobe Photoshop Elements. This product is considered the entry-level product in Adobe's graphics lineup, but the truth is that you can create "a lot of damage" using this tool as an alternative to the higher-end Photoshop. For beginners, it can be easily mastered in a relatively short amount of time.

There are other Adobe products that designers use, such as Illustrator and InDesign. If you know these products or have the time to learn them, go for it. But you can actually get by with just Photoshop or Photoshop Elements for creating your band's graphics.

Digital Cameras

By the time you finish this paragraph, prices on digital cameras will have dropped by some percentage point. That's how quickly digital camera technology has both improved and come down in price. That's good news for you, because a digital camera, especially when combined with Photoshop, can create graphical wonders. The filters in Photoshop that create painterly effects or lighting effects and other magic can take an ordinary photograph to new levels. The effectiveness of all of this depends on your imagination and how well you can grasp a few Photoshop techniques.

The Studio, the Green Screen, and the Magician

If you happen to have a friend with a professional photography studio—a friend who is kind enough to let you use it for a day—you can get wonderful results from studio lighting, reflectors, tripods, and other available equipment. In addition to that, the studio may be set up with a scrim. A *scrim* is a cloth curtain that hangs from the ceiling down to the floor—and continues on the floor to the foreground, creating a continuous, seamless look. You've probably seen models being photographed in front of a scrim in a studio. If you or your band uses this type of setup, you can immediately elevate your photo session to a professional level.

The green screen is another technique used in film, video, and sometimes photo sessions. By shooting a subject in front of a green screen and then using the correct filters, you can easily add any type of background to a scene later on in post-production. This is the technique that helps Superman or Spider-Man fly around the city with ease.

But Photoshop can also come to the rescue in this area. With careful selection of the foreground element (which may be you) during the editing process, you can also place any type of background behind a subject by eliminating the original background. And again, this technique is completely available in Photoshop Elements. A good grasp of Photoshop can help you create graphics that are useful for all of your merchandise.

Using Contractors for Implementing Graphics

If you're nervous about the prospect of creating logos and other graphic elements, you're probably not alone. The last thing you want is to do something subpar, mainly because you might not have the chops to do the graphics work. Presentation, as they say, is everything. Don't cut yourself short by settling for something that doesn't scream professional, hot, contemporary, and memorable.

Graphic artists are magicians with images, just as you are with music. There's no shame in letting a good artist jam with images of your act. With the right graphic artist, the results can be fantastic.

Graphic Pitfalls You Should Avoid Whether you decide to create the graphic elements yourself or hire a professional artist to do it, there are some common pitfalls to avoid that can make your presentation less than professional. This applies to logos, web pages, album art, and anything else you use to promote yourself.

1. **Typeface overkill.** Just because your Mac or PC comes with a million type fonts, that doesn't mean you have to use all of them (or half of them or a quarter of them). Stick to two basic typefaces. One might be a sans serif type (such as Arial), and another could be a serif type (such as Times Roman). These two examples are commonly used—so you might decide to pick something else. But keep it to two or possibly three fonts.

2. **Image confusion.** Make sure that your graphic elements are relevant to your image or message. There might be elements that are related to your musical genre, and there might be other images that are unique to you. But if you create something too far out, people will not be able to relate to it—or to you.

3. **Too many pieces.** Remember that line from *Amadeus* in which the King doesn't like Mozart's music (or more correctly, he is *told* that he doesn't like Mozart's music). The king complained that there were "too many notes." Avoid using too many elements in your graphic design. As with fonts, focus on a couple or a few, so that people are not distracted. They're distracted enough as it is. Keep it simple.

4. **Another stock photo.** Question: How many websites contain too many stock photos? Answer: Tons of them. I suggest you avoid stock photos completely, lest you be confused with some other group, such as the PTA. With the amazing technology available to everyone today, from digital cameras to photo software, there's no excuse not to create something original and impactful.

How to Hire a Graphic Artist

If you decide to hire a graphic artist, she should be both an artist and a designer. Some graphic artists are good with lots of direction. But designers have a certain knack for how to realize your vision—both conceptually and practically.

1. **Ask for recommendations.** Ask your friends, relatives, and acquaintances for referrals. Ask professional printers you may have used. Use the web for a targeted search. Decide whether the designer should be in your geographical area (which is usually a good idea if you want one-on-one meetings). Use Craigslist. Use your instincts. And when you've identified someone, ask to see his portfolio (online or physical).

2. **Carefully review the artist's portfolio.** Does she have the right sensibilities? Has she done previous work that lends itself to the job at hand? Does the portfolio knock your socks off? If it doesn't, you might want to keep looking.

3. **Interview the graphic artist.** Ask a few questions. If he's good, he will ask *you* a lot of questions. He might want to hear your music—and he should.

4. **Get a bid.** You might get two or three or four bids, depending on how many candidates you've found. Make sure the estimate includes everything—and this may vary widely depending on whether the designer is just designing and leaving the rest up to you (printing, creating the actual merchandise, and so on).

5. **Get a contract.** Even a simple one- or two-page contract is better than nothing. Search the web for some example contracts and draft one that is specific to your needs. Designate payments in steps, such as half of the payment up front and half upon completion of the project. You'll thank me later. (You're welcome.)

6. **Create review milestones along the way.** Don't wait until the end of the design process to say "I love it" or "I hate it." Check the progress along the way and make suggestions or shout out compliments, as appropriate. It should be an interactive process.

7. **Review the final product.** Break out the champagne. (But deliver the final payment first.)

There may be variations on this plan according to your specific needs. If you're insecure or unsure of whether the artist is appropriate for your project, he's probably not.

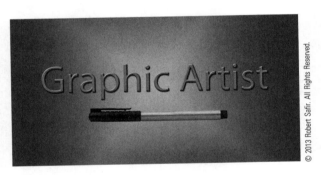

Types of Merchandise for Musicians (and Their Fans)

There are types of merchandise that are proven to work in the context of musicians and budding artists. Naturally, the first that comes to mind is the T-shirt. An anthropologist in the year 3012 might look back at artifacts of our day and become convinced that the T-shirt was the most common piece of clothing in our day—and it would be a T-shirt with some sort of writing and graphics displayed on the front and possibly the back. Most of these T-shirts would be related to musical groups or recording artists. Perhaps this anthropologist will find one of *your* T-shirts.

Although it has been done over and over, the T-shirt remains a staple of a musician's arsenal of merchandise.

The Ubiquitous, Universal, Undying T-Shirt

Let's be honest. How many T-shirts do you have in your drawer or closet? (Or should I say drawers and closets?) Aside from being highly practical as casual wear and perfect for dressing in layers, we become attached to T-shirts because of the idea, emotion, group, company, or revolution that the T-shirt might represent. And once we've committed ourselves to a concept or celebrity by purchasing that T-shirt, we tend to hold onto the shirt until the colors are faded and it is three sizes too small.

What a perfect vehicle for merchandise for an up-and-coming artist!

So how do you go about creating a T-shirt for yourself or your act? First, I will go on the basic assumption that you have already created your logo or your artwork, as discussed earlier in this chapter. Next, you need to look at the options for the type of T-shirt you will make.

Silkscreen

A silkscreen is a print made using a stencil process in which an image or design is superimposed on a very fine mesh screen. Then, printing ink is "squeegeed" onto the printing surface through the area of the screen not covered by the stencil. Silkscreen is not a new technique (it has been around for hundreds of years), but it became a very popular way of creating T-shirts in the 1960s and 1970s. Silkscreen is a technique best used for creating large quantities of T-shirts, but with a limited number of colors.

Digital Printing

Digital printing is a "direct to T-shirt" method that is effective for small quantities but can support full-color photographs with numerous colors. It works best on cotton fabrics.

Embroidery

Embroidery requires lots of stitching, takes a lot of time, and costs a lot of money. It looks great, but you might want to reserve this technique for your own personal leather jacket.

It comes down to two basic choices:

If You're Making	Then Choose
Large quantities with limited colors	Silkscreen
Small quantities, full-color photos	Digital

How to Print the T-Shirts

There are literally tons (okay, they don't *weigh* tons, but there's a lot of them) of places across the United States to get T-shirts created. There are huge printing plants that are not necessarily located in large cities. You can be in the middle of Kansas and find a great manufacturer of custom T-shirts (and indeed, there are some great printers in Kansas).

If you don't have a local resource, do not fear. The method used most often in the twenty-first century is *online*. The shop that popularized the printing of T-shirts (and other merchandise) is called CafePress (www.cafepress.com).

If you go to CafePress, click on the top menu item on the right: Design Your Own. This will give you a drop-down menu that includes much more than just T-shirts. There are mugs, hats, bags, stickers, hoodies, iPhone cases, and a whole lot more.

The neat thing about the "design your own" concept is that you can try ideas out before you settle on a final direction. This concept is not limited to CafePress. Lots of online resources include this functionality, including the Graphic Edge, CustomInk.com, Zazzle.com, and a whole lot more. And like CafePress, they are not limited to just T-shirts.

Where to Print the T-Shirts

Now, the thing to keep in mind here is that these sites might provide a good method of trying out your ideas online. The drawback is that their prices can be fairly high, with regular T-shirts costing in the range of $25 to $30 each. So you might want to consider using a website for testing out your graphic ideas on a "virtual product" and then seeing whether you can locate a printer with more aggressive pricing—depending, of course, on the quantity of products you plan to create.

Open Your Own Online Store

That said, the *advantage* of a website such as CafePress is that you can create your own virtual store online and provide a link to your fans for buying merchandise there. You will want to have a slight markup so that the effort produces some sort of revenue. CafePress offers both basic shops that are free and premium shops costing $4.99 per month with custom web layouts and a more professional shopping experience. Either way, all transactions are handled for you and include secure checkout and credit card processing.

Other Products You Can Create and Sell

The list is endless, as they say. But merchandise to consider includes:

- Limited-edition T-shirts (small print run, higher profit for you)
- Hoodies
- Hats
- Visors
- Sweats
- Mugs
- Water bottles
- Thermos bottles
- iPhone cases
- iPad cases
- Any kind of cases
- Mouse pads
- Magnets
- Posters
- Beanies
- Clocks
- Stickers
- Notebooks
- And more…

I am not exaggerating when I say "And more…." Just a quick glance at the offerings from CafePress (see Figure 8.1) gives you an idea of many of the merchandising ideas available.

And don't forget digital merchandise, such as:

- Screensavers
- Wallpaper
- Ringtones

Creating these digital products takes a little bit of technical prowess. Yet, there are many "how to" guidelines in magazines, in books, and on the web. If you don't feel confident enough to create digital products like the ones mentioned above, find someone on your team who can do so or contract it out to someone else entirely. And anyone who is versatile enough to create or update websites is technical enough to produce digital merchandise.

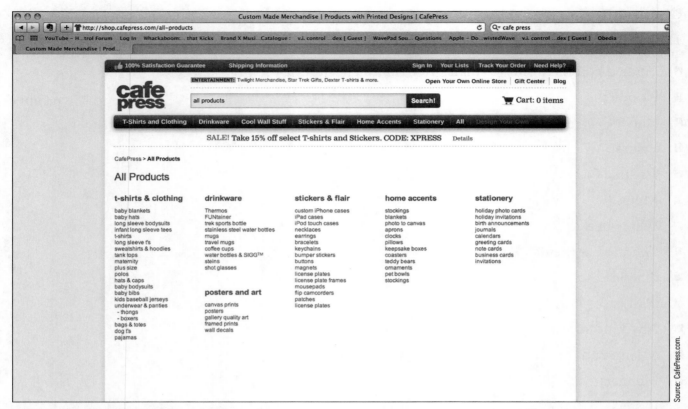

Figure 8.1 This screenshot from the CafePress website shows the large variety of products you can brand using your own artwork.

How and Where to Sell Your Merchandise

You may have gone to concerts where there are booths sporting the band's CDs and other merchandise. They are usually the busiest after the concert is over, assuming that the music was good. This is a natural place for you to sell merchandise, with the ubiquitous T-shirt selling right next to your latest CD.

The three main places you might sell your merchandise are your:

■ Concerts

■ Website

■ Hosted online store

Pricing and Promotion

Some of the hosted online stores determine not only the cost to you, but what the markup should be, such as 10 percent. In other cases, you can determine the cost to your fans yourself. But don't give it away unless you want to use merchandise for promotion.

Giveaways, contests, and other promotions are a perfect vehicle for your merchandise. You simply need to consider how much you're willing to give away and when. In merchandising language, you have a "loss leader" in which you are directly taking the hit on manufacturing costs, but it's for a good purpose—including the prospect of enticing fans to buy more.

Included in this concept is your music itself. A free CD or download can be used as a promotional item and may be a better reward for lots of your fans.

Just don't overdo the "free" thing.

Learn from the Masters

When you go to a concert, observe how the artists are marketing and merchandising their act.

When you visit a website, study the ways in which merchandise is promoted or sold, when it's sold, and how it's promoted.

When you go to an online store, the virtual storefront for a band or act, take note of what they're doing right—and what they're doing wrong, if anything.

In short, learn from the masters—those who are successful acts and have a following. They may be a Billboard Top 10 group or a newly arrived independent artist. Whatever the case, pull back the camera (your own virtual camera) far enough to objectively study what they do.

This will provide you with a terrific learning experience—and best of all, it's free.

9 Other Business Considerations of Music Merchandising

While a complete understanding of the legal and business issues of the music business is beyond the scope of this book, there are a few things I'd like to mention in relation to the marketing and merchandising of your music. If you do want to delve into the business intricacies of the music biz, there are plenty of great books available. And don't forget the web—you can search on any topic and find a wealth of information. (Just make sure to cross-check it if you can—many people have the mistaken assumption that if it's on the Internet, then it must be true!)

Using Outside Resources

There are several aspects of merchandising that you might choose to outsource or contract. Professional merchandisers and events planners are two that immediately come to mind.

Professional Merchandisers

There are both individuals and companies that are positioned as professional merchandisers. They are often the people who not only develop merchandising concepts, but help set up retail and POP (*point-of-purchase*) displays for increasing sales in the stores.

Professional merchandisers might be of assistance to you when you are far enough along in your music career to warrant hiring them. You should have a good enough (and objective enough) grasp of where you are on the success ladder to know the answer to this question. If you're not sure, then you're probably not ready for a professional merchandiser.

The techniques described in this book have focused around DIY (*do-it-yourself*) methods and/or the prospect of hiring graphic designers and artists to help implement your ideas. Toss in professional print shops that can save you money if you're printing merchandise in large enough quantities—and add online stores such as CafePress and others who can help you set up a virtual store—and you likely will have your bases covered. If you need something on a more massive scale, then perhaps you *are* ready to hire a professional merchandiser.

Event Planners

There are professional event planners who can help customers with weddings, bar mitzvahs, graduation parties, and similar events.

If you are far enough along in your career that you are staging concerts and road tours of some sort, then an event planner could be appropriate.

Event planning can include budgeting, establishing schedules (as well as alternate dates), reserving the location, and acquiring the necessary permits. But event planners may also be responsible for establishing a theme for a prospective event, determining what décor might be appropriate, creating signage for the location, and handling other responsibilities that clearly encroach upon the tasks involved in marketing and merchandising your music.

As is the case in making a decision to hire a professional merchandiser, you need to assess where you are in your career and whether you need to contract out this function. Also, as is often the case, your decision will be largely guided by your budget (which I'll get back to later in the "Finances" section).

Getting Permission—and Other Legalities

Oh yeah, the legal stuff. Are you the type of person who hates to deal with these matters or figures you'll deal with them later? I hope not. This is the type of stuff that can come back later and bite you in the—well, you get the idea.

If you can't deal with the legal stuff, maybe someone in your circles can. But for now, let me cover a few things related to the topic of this book.

Using Stock Photography

In the previous chapter, I strongly dissuaded you from using stock photography—and for good reason. (Go back and reread Chapter 8 if you need to!) However, if you *did* decide to use stock photography, refrain from doing the following. Do not:

- Use stock photography without the necessary clearances
- Use photographs downloaded from the web without permission

Sure, there are quick and easy ways to obtain stock photographs if you decide to use them. But here's a guiding rule: Don't do anything of an illegal nature that you wouldn't want people to do when it comes to your music. Get the picture? This rule makes a lot of sense.

Remember, too, that if you use *original* photographs involving people other than yourself, get the necessary releases from the people in the images. Oh, they're your friends, you say? That doesn't matter. Maybe they won't be your friend two years from now—and you'll be using their photograph without permission. You can easily find photo releases by searching the web. Then you can customize them to suit your specific purpose.

Copyrighting and Trademarking Your Own Material

Let's look at this from the opposite perspective. Say you've gone through all of the trouble of creating artwork and merchandise based upon your ideas and those of the people you hired. You've invested a lot of time—and some amount of money—to realize your vision and create the final products. But you don't think it's necessary to copyright or trademark any of the materials.

Then that nasty ex-friend of yours, two years from now, decides to use some or all of the materials that you did not legally protect. And there you have it. Good luck trying to defend your legal rights.

You know how to copyright your music, so take the time to learn how to copyright printed materials or trademark logos. You'll thank me later. If you're interested in a book on the subject, check out *Music Copyright Law* (Course Technology PTR, 2012).

Contracts

Say you've been in a band for three years, and you're finally getting some traction. Suppose you've got the live-concert thing going, you've created a logo, and you've implemented a lot of great merchandise. Everything is looking rosy.

But say your nasty friend is also the bass player who gets replaced a year from now. Or possibly, *you're* the one who gets replaced next month.

What contracts spell out who has what share of what merchandise? How much is that share worth? Who invested what monies to create the merchandise in the first place? How do band members (or investors, if they're involved) get paid?

You go through the trouble of creating contracts when you co-write or co-publish songs, don't you? (Umm…don't you?)

You need to cover all the legal bases with all of your creative materials—from participation in songs and publishing, to shares of revenue created by your merchandise.

If you don't feel comfortable doing that, you might consider hiring a professional, which brings me to my next subject.

Lawyers

First, no lawyer jokes. Everyone has heard them all, and they belong in some other book, not this one. Besides, we're serious here about possibly needing an attorney. So think about it for a minute.

A lot of what I described earlier regarding permissions, copyrights, trademarks, and contracts can possibly be handled by you and some excellent skills in searching the web. This, combined with the ability to customize verbiage for your own specific needs, could yield some legal papers that are tight enough to get you through. I say, *could* yield. Then again, maybe not. This is a decision you need to make.

If you decide to hire a lawyer to assist you in these endeavors, make sure you hire a music lawyer. The lawyer who got your cousin an accident settlement when she was rear-ended is not the right guy for this gig. The music business has its own unique set of rules, regulations, and idiosyncrasies.

That said, a music business lawyer who meets your needs and can work within your budget is a valuable asset. Which brings me to my next topic…

Finances

Have you ever seen that cartoon illustration that says "Plan Ahead," and there's no room on the page for the "d" at the end of the sentence? You haven't? Well, you get the idea, right?

Finances can spin out of control when you or your band is making progress in leaps and bounds. When you engage in the activities discussed in this book—whether you choose the DIY route or you use outside resources—you will run into some costs. If you use event planners and lawyers, you'll really run into some costs.

When you've done some of your original planning for marketing and merchandising, try to create a budget. As you move forward, record the "actuals" versus the budget amounts for the categories you've created. This is not an exact science, as some things will change in the course of your projects. Monitor and record those changes. You—or someone you designate—must keep track of expenses, especially when you start creating different types of merchandise. And as I mentioned earlier in the "Contracts" section, you will need to know who spent what on various projects so that these costs are reflected in your legal documents.

Investors

Do you have outside investors involved in your act? Did they front you some money so that you could cover the expenses mentioned in this book?

If so, re-read this chapter and multiply any scary parts by a factor of 10. If you think I've been strict in trying to get you to cover your legal bases, wait until you start dealing with your investors. Whew!

Whether they are your immediate or distant relatives, major or minor investment firms, make sure you have your contract deals nailed down and that you keep perfectly accurate records of your expenses. Because if you took the independent path as described in this book, *you are the record company.*

10 Latest Trends in Digital Music

Long ago, on a warm summer's day, I remember my parents bringing home a new appliance for playing records. It was a Webcor High Fidelity Stereo record player. Of those four words, *stereo* marked the big advancement in music listening pleasure. Two speakers hung off each side of the turntable, *and* they could be disconnected from the turntable to be placed farther apart, up to the length of the connecting cables. The difference between this listening experience and the old technology—mono—was mind-bending. Stereo was the mono killer. There was no more use for mono, with the exception of broadcasters who held onto it for some time because there were still car radios that could receive only mono AM stations. But for all intents and purposes, mono became as useful as 8-track music players (which also headed for the sunset as time moved on).

Webcor Hi-Fidelity Stereo (Mock-up)

As the saying goes, "All things change, but not all change is good." I don't know who actually said that, but it's a saying that is often relevant. And, there are a number of cases where it is irrelevant.

Change, especially in technology, has been a driving force in the latter part of the twentieth century and into the twenty-first. The other side of the coin when it comes to change is obsolescence. In that regard, the new makes the old obsolete—but not always. As is the case with many things, you must have an understanding of how things were done in the past so that you can understand the future.

In this chapter I will address some of the latest changes going on in the new music business, such as downloading and streaming. At the same time, I will address some of the *old* things going on in the music business so that you get an overall perspective of how some changes affect others. Some of these old things include royalty payments, mechanical rights, synchronizations rights, and so on.

The Music Biz: The Times Are Changing

The rate of change in the way we obtain and listen to music is so rapid that I've had to rewrite sections of this book during the writing process. Mind you, I don't mean the editing process, which comes later on, *after* the book is written. I literally mean that constant changes, with the aid of constant monitoring of music and technology news, have necessitated rewrites as I pound away on this keyboard on a chapter-by-chapter basis. That's fast!

To give you some additional perspective on this, consider the state of the music industry when Napster came onto the music scene, around the end of the 1990s:

- Music sales were dominated by CDs, accounting for approximately 90 percent of all music sales.
- Cassettes were still around, responsible for about 8 percent of recorded music sales.
- People weren't walking around with their iPods just yet, because there were no iPods yet!
- There was no MySpace, no Facebook, and no Twitter. No social networks existed.
- The major record labels were generating their best sales ever.
- People were *barely* beginning to download albums, singles, or anything for that matter.

After a relatively short time, the music industry barely resembles what it once was at that time.

The Forces at Play

The music world is currently upside down and backwards, not because one or two things are changing, but because many different forces and processes are at play.

Consider the following examples:

- The business model for artists, labels, and songwriters is in complete flux.
- The Internet has completely leveled the playing field for music creation and distribution.
- The record deal is no longer the Holy Grail for aspiring artists.
- The traditional music industry has declined by 71 percent in the last decade.
- YouTube has replaced MTV as the resource for music videos.
- Apple is the largest music retailer in the world.
- Artists and musicians can create masters in their bedrooms, and often do.
- People can instantly download music from a number of sources.
- People can instantly stream music from a lot of sources, many of which offer free music.
- The transition from analog to digital has enabled unlimited copying, sharing, purchasing single songs, building playlists, music portability, instant downloading, unlimited streaming, and a hundred other things that have changed the rules of the music industry.
- Payments to artists and songwriters from music downloading and streaming revenue are in a state of flux.
- The role of radio and its impact on record sales have been severely diminished.
- Advertising revenues for traditional media that promote music are in a downward spiral.
- There is no textbook for how to deal with this tumultuous change in the music business.

So, the changes in the music business run deep, run wide, and move very fast. To be competitive, you not only have to keep up with all of it, but you have to be ahead of the curve. That's not an easy task, to say the least.

Do You Want Fries with That?

Trends in today's online music companies would make a good ad for Burger King. Taking the concept of "Have it your way" to an extreme, every conceivable method for downloading, streaming, or otherwise acquiring music is being offered by both startups and major music online companies alike.

That being said, everything (as of this writing) seems to boil down to two major viewpoints on how music is delivered and consumed:

Do people want to *own* their music?

Or...

Do people simply want *access* to their music?

How Downloading Is Like Owning (Almost)

The later days of the last century saw digital music as a downloading experience. From the illegal downloading that began with Napster to the legal downloading of music that transformed the music business with iTunes, people could obtain music by downloading it to their computer's hard drive. Subsequent syncing to portable devices, such as the iPod, was still part of an overall downloading process. Music existed on servers and then was downloaded to computers and ultimately to portable devices. If you chose to include CDs you had already purchased in a store or online, then your own record collection was "uploaded" to your iTunes collection as well. These processes simply indicate the transferring of music files in one way or another.

Downloading music is equivalent to "owning" the music, just as people have owned records, cassettes, and CDs. Of course, consumers of music don't really own the *content* of the CD or digital file—they simply own the physical CD or the file on their computer or iPod. The subject of true music ownership is a whole other can of worms, complete with the complexities of copyright, creator's rights, publishing rights, mechanical rights, synchronization rights, and your right to remain silent. These concepts go well beyond the scope of this book, but they are subjects you really should research and study (including the right to remain silent).

As of this writing, downloading music is quickly becoming the main trend in music delivery and consumption. But this could possibly change in the near future.

How Streaming Is the Same as Access

Advances in computer bandwidth and transfer rates enabled the capability of streaming music from the Internet. Rather than the music file being stored permanently on your hard drive, you receive a "progressive download" that exists only during the time you're hearing the music. You can think of it as radio for the Internet. In fact, actual radio stations on the Internet are streaming music to you—you aren't downloading it onto your computer's hard drive.

Streaming music is a business model that states what people really want is *access* to their music. *Ownership* of the music (via downloading) is not really necessary. Of course, as I stated previously, you never actually own the music anyway. You might own the CD or music file that contains the music, but actual ownership belongs to the content originator—namely, the songwriter or artist. So by using the word *ownership*, we really mean *possession* of some type of media that contains music.

How Would You Like to Pay for That?

Another distinction between downloading and streaming is how payment is made for the music transaction. The downloading model is structured on paying for each "unit" of music. When iTunes was established, a single (whether a hit single or just an individual song) cost 99 cents. After a few years, the price was hiked to $1.29—still a good deal, especially when you consider that you're paying for songs you actually want, rather than songs that might happen to fill up an artist's album.

Some of the early downloading sites used a subscription model, rather than a pay-as-you-purchase concept. You could pay a monthly fee based upon either the number of songs you downloaded or perhaps the number of computers or mobile devices to which you could download the song. There were (and still are) tiered plans with different pricing models. On the low end, some services were free or $4.99 per month, and there were high-end offerings that cost about $14.99 per month. (The term "high end" is used liberally here. $14.99 is certainly not high end for a BMW, but a music service at $14.99 is high end when compared to a free one.)

Today we find ourselves at a virtual crossroads of digital music purchase and subscription models. From its inception, iTunes dominated the downloaded music market and took the position that people don't want to pay more monthly fees for a service. With iTunes dominating market share, competitors began to struggle for ways to stay alive in the marketplace. Although iTunes still dominates today, a new monkey wrench has been thrown into the system with technology advances in online storage and SaaS (*Software as a Service*).

A Change in Weather: Clouds in My Coffee

The big buzzword these days is all about the "cloud." Cloud computing is literally defined as "The practice of using a network of remote servers hosted on the Internet to store, manage, and process data, rather than a local server (or a personal computer)." Some people define cloud computing as applications and services offered over the Internet. The bottom line is that cloud computing—or cloud storage—means that the data is stored on remote servers, and the interface is (most often) a web browser.

As it applies to the music business, the music itself is stored on servers, and the interface is the way you obtain, play, and sometimes share the music—either through a web browser or an application. At the most basic level, the cloud is simply a place to store your music.

Recently, companies have either started new companies with cloud-based music services or created cloud-based music services from their existing downloading sites. As of today, iTunes is a downloading site that has just launched a cloud-based service, Apple iCloud, and chances are that both models will coexist for some time to come.

The Big Three in the Cloud

As of today, there are three major players in the area of "music in the cloud." They are:

- Amazon's Cloud Player
- Google Music
- Apple iCloud

All three services are similar but not exactly the same. The biggest difference between Apple iCloud and the others is that it's not only for storing music. Its functions include email, contacts, and calendar—as well as syncing up photos and other data stored on other Apple devices.

In addition, iCloud requires using iTunes or some other Apple iOS device—you can't play songs using a web browser (as you can by using Amazon's Cloud Player or Google Music). Of course, you could use iTunes on a PC that runs Windows, but other than that, it's Apple all the way.

Another difference is that, technically, Apple doesn't stream the songs from its servers—they are downloaded to your computer or portable device for playback. However, Apple has around 20 million tracks already stored on its servers. This means you won't have to upload most of your music collection once Apple checks to see that you already "own" that song. With the other services, you have to upload your music collection, which can be a tedious process if you have a large collection.

Apple has a track record of signing up the major labels with distribution deals, and thus has the largest catalog offering of music. Apple also has a unique feature called iTunes Match. With it, you pay $24.99 a year to store music that was not purchased on iTunes. However, once you pay that fee, your storage space is virtually unlimited. The other services are not concerned with where or how you acquired your music.

This is a distinction to be aware of—for it is highly likely that your music was not purchased on iTunes (not by you, anyway). There is also the matter of storing many variations of one of your tracks in progress—a project you're working on—and you may want access to it on a number of computers or devices. Still, we're only talking about $24.99 per year, so it's not a major drawback.

One other consideration has to do with the file types that are supported. Apple's iCloud has the most (and best) selection, including MP3, AIFF, WAV, MPEG-4, and AAC. The other two offerings are limited in this area, which is not a major concern for music consumers—but it could be for a music creator, such as yourself.

Some analysts are predicting that cloud-based music services will be mainstream by 2016, driven mainly by mobile music devices (primarily smartphones). These same analysts are predicting that the primary beneficiaries of the cloud-based music services will be the service providers themselves, and to some extent, the record labels (if there are any). The troubling piece is that music creators may get the short end of the stick, with growing expectations by both consumers and music companies that royalty rates for music creators should continue to fall. This is troubling indeed, as the current rates are extremely low right now. I'll discuss various artist rights and declining royalties throughout this chapter.

Sync Whole

A convenience feature that these cloud makers offer is the ability to sync your music on your various devices without fumbling with one USB cable. Further, your music gets synced to all of your devices (if you so choose—and you usually do) at the same time. This is where the term "the cloud" seems much more like, well, a cloud. It happens somewhere "in the air," or so it seems.

For you, the music creator, it makes your life much simpler. You're in a hurry, you do a quick reference mix of the latest track you're working on, you put it on iTunes or whatever Android cloud service you choose, and before you even get to your car to deposit your royalties in the bank, your latest reference track is ready to be played on your iPhone (or Android phone or whatever-phone).

The Growing Lineup of Online Music Sites

If it seems as if every day there are more and more online music sites, that's because every day there are more and more online music sites. Some are inventive; others are copycats. Some are on a mission to provide music creators with more tools to market themselves and their music, while others are opportunistic, simply attempting to cash in on a good thing. Some have been started by musicians who were fed up with the music business of old, while others have been launched by opportunists who see a way to make a quick buck. (Wait until this latter group finds out that nobody wants to pay decent money for music anymore!)

You will need to research, investigate, and navigate the ever-growing lineup of online music sites to determine which ones fit your needs.

Some sites are music-downloading sites and some are streaming sites, as discussed in the beginning of this chapter. But it is more complicated than that. Some sites are designed to stream original music for emerging artists like you. Others are online music sites that act as "radio stations," streaming a variety of music for the benefit of their target market. Still others are streaming video, not music (per se). Still others act as aggregators, "middlemen" that act on your behalf to get your music placed on a variety of sites. There are direct-to-fan sites, platforms for artists and labels to engage with fans and sell music and merchandise online or in conjunction with another site, such as Facebook. And then there are music "pitching" services, providing you with opportunities to place your music in a television show, film, or commercial, either for a one-time fee or a monthly subscription to their service.

A Partial List

Because of rapid changes in the music business, some of these sites straddle more than one category or completely change their business model from one category to another. So, in no particular order, here are online music sites that fall into these various groups:

- iTunes
- Spotify
- Rhapsody
- Napster
- AOL Radio
- iLike
- Last.fm
- Pandora
- Grooveshark
- YouTube
- SoundCloud
- Slacker
- Blip.fm
- Turntable.fm
- Swift.fm
- 8tracks
- Hype Machine
- MOG
- Nimbit
- ReverbNation
- Band Jam
- Google Music
- MySpace Music
- Facebook
- Broadjam
- Taxi
- Sonicbids
- Music Xray
- Bandit
- Audio Rokit
- Apple iCloud

- Amazon Cloud
- Google Cloud
- And many more

Because of the number of sites and the variety of services they offer, it would be advisable to study the ones you like and to understand as much as you can about any and all legal issues involved with that company. These issues can deal with copyright, licensing, royalties, and a whole host of legal rights, such as performance rights, mechanical rights, synchronization rights, and more.

Call My Lawyer

The legalities involved in streaming, downloading, and cloud storage, not to mention the royalties attached to each of these, are so confusing that even your lawyer may not understand what's going on. I'm not saying this to be facetious. These matters have become so complex—and nebulous at the same time—that a lot of these legal issues are still open to interpretation.

As a music creator, this concerns you. You need to keep abreast of these developments and how they affect you. The days of the record company taking care of it are long gone. You said you wanted to DIY (do it yourself), didn't you?

There are currently a few legal challenges (and sometimes, just power challenges) going on in the world of downloading and streaming music—mostly related to artists (such as Coldplay and the Black Keys) that do not like the miniscule royalties being paid by services (such as Spotify, Rdio, and Rhapsody). These artists aren't fond of having their music posted without permission, either. Coldplay and the Black Keys pulled their song catalogs from Spotify as a way of showing how dissatisfied they really were.

The royalties paid from Spotify and similar services are low because, according to them, subscriber levels are just starting to build, and they hope that many of Spotify's free subscribers will switch to their enhanced premium (paid) service. Spotify claims that if and when paid subscribers increase, so too will the royalty payments. How likely is this to happen? Please go back and read this book from Page 1 if you don't know the answer.

These scenarios have not fully played out yet. Remember, we're in a transition period, so it's anybody's best guess as to how royalties will ultimately be structured for downloading, streaming, cloud storage, and so on—and how these monies will be paid to artists, songwriters, musicians, labels, indie labels, producers, and others involved in the creative process. Time will tell.

Understanding Your Rights—and Royalties

In one corner, you have performing rights organizations, such as ASCAP, BMI, and SESAC. Then there are the people that collect "mechanicals"—the Harry Fox Agency (more on mechanicals in a minute). There are also independent companies involved in calculating and/or distributing royalties, such as Music Reports and SoundExchange.

It is critical that you have some understanding of your rights as a content creator and the respective royalties that are attached to different media. Without this, you are certain to lose out. Most companies are not lining up to make sure you have every penny coming to you in royalties, and indeed, it is pennies we're talking about (that quickly add up to dollars).

Because there are so many types of media now—and because of the rights and royalties assigned to new media in particular—it is imperative to comprehend both the old and new music trends.

You Have the Right to Remain Silent (but Don't)

An understanding of music rights, licenses, and royalties can quickly get very confusing. There are several layers of copyright law that apply to music, some of which apply to the song itself, the recording of the song, the performance of it (in a radio/TV broadcast or in a public place), or the licensing of the rights to use the music in synchronization with visuals. In a discussion of music marketing and merchandising, such as the subject of this book, a basic understanding of these rights is necessary so that you understand what you can and cannot do with your music. The rights to your music begin the moment you create your music, but how your music is used from that point forward varies widely. From time to time, you may need to speak out (or have your lawyer do so, if you have one) so that your rights and royalties are protected.

Here is a rundown of some of the rights involved in the world of music:

- **Synchronization Rights.** This is the right to use music in timed relations with another visual element, such as a film, video, television show, or other audio/visual production. Synchronization licenses are obtained from the publisher songwriter/composer of the music if a publisher is not already involved.

- **Master Use Rights.** This is the right to use the master—the final, mixed production of the song or track, and it is also protected by copyright. A record label usually owns this copyright and can grant the right to use the recording in an album or an audio/visual medium. This is basically the right to use the master sound recording.

- **Performing Rights.** Every time a song is performed on a radio or television broadcast, there is a public performance involved. This public performance is licensed by performing rights organizations (PRO), such as ASCAP or BMI, or directly from the copyright holder as a direct license.

- **Mechanical Rights.** This is the right to use a song owned by someone else in a recording. The license is granted at an agreed-upon fee per unit sold.

- **Direct License.** This is a license obtained directly from the copyright owner or publisher where the licensee pays the performing rights directly to the copyright owner. In this case, no royalties are collected by or paid to the PRO.

- **Copyright.** This is the exclusive right, granted by law for a stated period (usually until 70 years after the death of the surviving author of the work), to create and otherwise control copies of musical and other copyrightable works.

Of all these rights, copyright is the most basic and important right to understand, and in fact it affects all of the other rights included in this list.

Understanding PROs (Performing Rights Organizations)

PROs are performing rights organizations. They license broadcasters—such as radio and television networks—so that shows airing on their respective stations can air music during programs, such as *Dancing with the Stars*, *American Idol*, or *Diary of a Teenage Werewolf*. When television shows such as these air music, producers are responsible for tracking the names of songs (or tracks), how this music is used, and the track's running time. The resulting cue sheets are forwarded to PROs, such as ASCAP or BMI. The cue sheets are the primary way that PROs keep track of music on television and distribute their licensing revenue to songwriters and composers. If any of your music is used in these shows, you will receive royalties from the performing rights organization with which you are affiliated.

Performance revenue is not the same as mechanical revenue. Mechanicals refer to the physical formats that carry the music, such as CDs (and in the "old days," LPs, cassettes, 8-track tapes, and so on). The Harry Fox Agency is the organization that collects and distributes royalties for unit sales such as the ones mentioned here.

Digital Transmissions

Just when you thought it was safe to get your music played over the airwaves, along comes digital transmission to make things more complicated.

If you have a grasp on how royalties are paid in the "old" music business, then it is time to sit down (and I *do* recommend sitting down) and get caught up on digital transmissions in the "new" music business.

As you already know, when music is played on "old technology," such as AM or FM radio, the songwriter or composer is paid a royalty for the public performance of his song, which is usually monitored and collected by a PRO.

Digital transmissions, on the other hand, are mostly transmitted via the Internet, such as the music streamed and heard on Pandora. However, the list of streaming music services is growing very rapidly—you can immediately include Spotify, Apple iCloud, Amazon Cloud, and Google Music to this list. Actually, you could add dozens more, but these are examples that immediately come to mind. Other non-interactive music services include Sirius Satellite Radio or the music services provided through cable television.

Royalties through SoundExchange

Music streaming services provide detailed logs so that another company, SoundExchange, can pay out royalties earned by the specific parties involved in the production of the music.

SoundExchange monitors and collects money for music that comes under the heading of non-interactive digital transmissions. Essentially, this means that SoundExchange is the agency that pays performers, songwriters, and record labels when your music is streamed from a service such as Pandora. Because it is streamed, it is non-interactive, whereas music plays on sites such as MySpace or YouTube are defined as interactive, because users can specify exactly which tracks they want to stream.

Spotify and the Disappearing Penny

It's free to register with SoundExchange so that you may collect past or future royalties due to you from your non-interactive, digitally streamed music. But before you get excited and put a down payment on that new Mercedes, consider the royalty rate that Spotify, for example, pays for each play:

> You, the artist, will receive $0.00029 per play.

That means if your song plays 10,000 times, you will receive $2.90. Let me spell that out for you: *two dollars and ninety cents*.

Comparatively, 10,000 track downloads on iTunes generates close to $6,000.

Quick Review and Lessons Learned

If you thought royalties were low in the good ol' analog days, you ain't seen nothin' yet!

If you were planning to make a living from streaming music sales, fuhgeddaboudit!

These are sobering statistics, are they not? In one way, however, these very low rates aren't surprising—there has been a downhill slide in the royalties that songwriters and artists are entitled to for years. Therefore, extremely small figures, calculated in fractions of a penny, aren't that ridiculous. Well, okay—on second thought, these numbers *are* ridiculous.

The Pandora's Box of Pandora Radio

Pandora describes itself as follows: "*Pandora* radio is the personalized Internet radio service that helps you find new music based on your old and current favorites." Using Pandora, you can create "radio stations" based upon an artist you like, and Pandora will play similar music based upon your selected artist. The service is considered "non-interactive" in that you do not have the freedom to choose which song (or songs) comes up next in the queue. That's Pandora's job.

It is also Pandora's job to serve up lots of ads unless you pay for the premium service, which costs $36 per year. This upgrade also provides listeners with a higher bit rate (192 kbps) and a custom music player in place of the standard web browser.

Recent years have seen bitter fights involving Pandora, SoundExchange, record labels, artists, and songwriters to determine a "fair" royalty rate for all involved. As of today, Pandora explains the way royalties are handled as follows:

> There are two types of royalties for music played on streaming websites such as Pandora: performance royalties (for the performers of the music) and publishing royalties (for the writers/

owners of the music). Pandora pays statutory performance royalties to SoundExchange, as well as publishing royalties to ASCAP, SESAC, and BMI.

Many musicians are familiar with ASCAP, SESAC, and BMI, but unfamiliar with SoundExchange. To register with SoundExchange, please visit http://blog.pandora.com/info/contents/soundexchangeregistration.html [Author's note: you can also simply go to www.soundexchange.com to register—without any reference to Pandora radio.]

Artists and record labels can register with SoundExchange to collect their portion of the royalties paid by Pandora and other Internet Radio streamers. Similarly, songwriters collect their publishing royalties from ASCAP, SESAC, or BMI. They are negotiated separately by all legal music services including Pandora.

The larger mystery here is what the exact royalty rates are that Pandora pays to SoundExchange and the PROs. Further, it is a mystery as to the exact rate that the PROs pay to songwriters, composers, and lyricists for *regular broadcast performances*. Much of this information is shrouded in mystery: special formulas, algorithms, and other secret sauce—all of it not directly accessible to the artist (you).

Does this seem fair? Okay, sorry—dumb question.

There was a loud outcry from record labels when YouTube (Google) was making money off of the backs of the label's catalogs without paying royalties to the record companies.

Back-room deals have been made to satisfy the needs of labels and of executives in the new Internet music companies. These companies and executives are making a lot of money off of music products. What percentage of these revenues goes to you, the artist?

When you find out, please let me know. But I digress...

The End Is Just Beginning

Speaking of Pandora's Box, the original meaning of the fable applies, unfortunately, to current trends in artist and songwriter royalties.

Pandora's Box was opened the day that Internet content was deemed "free" by thousands of pimple-faced, ADHD-prone teenage boys who saw no reason for artists to have a right to make a living. If these children couldn't easily obtain content for free, then they would simply steal it. But again, they didn't consider it actually stealing, because the Internet was free.

Ah—but you say look at Internet radio and all of the other Internet music companies that are paying (ridiculously low) royalties to artists and songwriters. It can only get better, right?

Wrong.

Some of those people grew up to be greedy owners of Internet music startups. Perhaps YouTube (Google) decided to go straight and work within the system, but the young hoodlums will continue to do everything in their power to make sure you, the artist, do not get paid, even if it is a paltry royalty amount.

Actually, it's much worse than that.

In the old music business, guys wearing suits with chains around their necks and women on their arms would convince struggling artists that anything they do, including recording and touring, would be very good for their "exposure," which is why they shouldn't complain about performing for free.

Today, the younger jeans-and-T-shirt moguls will also try to convince you to do things for free because it is good for your exposure.

What's next? Having you pay them to play your music?

Yes, and it is already being done.

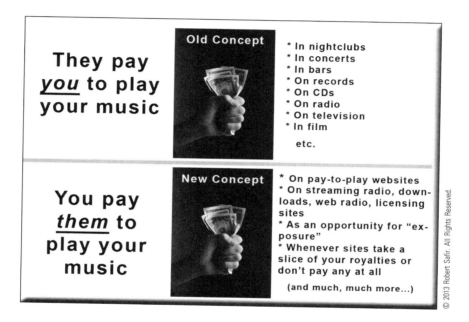

Up-and-coming artists (like you) are actually forfeiting their SoundExchange royalties (so that the startup can "cover their costs"), and SoundExchange is charging the artist or band two cents per play. It's good for you! It's exposure.

If you get such an offer, run for the hills—and hope that your peers run with you. If it continues, this trend cannot have a good ending. The only way to change this possible outcome is to stand up for your rights—not give them away.

But wait, there's more! Not to be outdone as new technology companies rob artists of their royalties and rights, record companies now offer some artists the *360 Deal*. The record company agrees to provide funds for the artist, including advances and monies for marketing, promotion, and touring. In return, the record company gets a piece of all of the action—everything that the artist does. (Do you get why it's called a "360 Deal?") The motivation for this is simple—the record companies are eager to grab any type of revenue possible, which gives them more artistic control at the same time. The whole idea is ironic for two reasons:

1. Record companies have been engaging in these types of activities for years, so much that this "new" 360 Deal is not very different from record deals of the past, such as those from Motown Records.

2. Record companies are encouraging the very behavior they're trying to prevent: artists abandoning labels for their own self-preservation, and the demise of record companies in general, giving rise to the so-called "new" music business.

The Future of Copyright

In case you haven't noticed by now, a lot of the issues that crop up when discussing digital music have to do with copyright, or the lack of it. Illegal downloading, pirating, file sharing, and a lot of other topics in the world of digital music should be of great concern to you as a content creator. Your future literally depends on it. In a world without copyright protection, your music royalties from streaming, downloading, and other forms of music distribution would amount to zero. (Some would argue that music royalties amount to zero right now, even *with* copyright protection.)

You Don't Own Me

There is a lot of history about copyright law, but never has it been brought to center stage in the way that the Internet has affected these issues. You can go back to the DMCA (Digital Millennium Copyright Act) of 1998 to see how the chasm has developed between content creators and Internet companies. The DMCA supposedly provided copyright protection by heightening penalties for copyright infringement on the Internet. This sounds good, except for the fact that this legislation limited the liability of online service providers for *any* copyright infringement by their users. The DMCA let Internet companies off the hook for any copyright infringement in the hope that new markets would be created without the restraints of outmoded copyright law.

Source: Digital Millennium Copyright Act. RIAA.

On the other end of the spectrum, copyright law *enforcement* has been made to look ridiculous by clumsy attempts at control, from plans to insert spyware onto your PC that deletes unauthorized music files, to outright lawsuits by the RIAA against consumers who engaged in illegal music downloads.

And so today there are two camps—one that wants to preserve the copyrights of content creators and another that says any attempts to do so amount to the outright destruction of the "free" Internet. These two camps have been at odds for more than a decade, and the battle continues to intensify. If you are an artist, songwriter, musician, or composer—and I assume you are—then the outcome of these arguments will affect you directly.

SOPA and PIPA

The issues involving copyright protection for digital music came to a head in January 2012, when various factions of the music and Internet industries engaged in a knock-down, drag-out fight over two proposed pieces of legislation—SOPA and PIPA. While these might sound like two types of an Italian dinner, they actually stand for the "Stop Online Privacy Act" and the "Protect IP Act," respectively.

The original intent of these bills was to stop foreign websites (such as the Pirate Bay and Mega-upload) from engaging in online commerce by using pirated content. Although the House and Senate bills are similar, SOPA is a bit more extreme, as it defines a "foreign infringing site" as any site that is "committing or facilitating" copyright infringement. PIPA is limited to sites with "no significant use other than" copyright infringement.

Opponents of the legislation argued that neither piece of legislation did enough to protect ISPs and websites from false accusations. The potential for abusing these proposed laws was high, they claimed, while immunity was very low. ISPs did not want the responsibility of monitoring the millions of pieces of content and then going after the violators of copyright law.

SOPA and PIPA would give the U.S. attorney general power to make payment networks and ad networks cut off funding to overseas websites accused of piracy.

Proponents of the legislation were worried that copyright owners were losing millions of dollars in potential revenue (let alone having their rights violated) and that jobs would be lost as well. The opponents of SOPA and PIPA took their complaints to the Internet, and in January 2012, some sites threatened to "go dark" (shut down or block access for a certain amount of time). These sites included Google, Wikipedia, Mozilla (Firefox), and many others.

The problem is that the opponents took their argument to extreme proportions, stating that these laws signified "the end of the Internet as we know it" and that there would be no more "free and open web," due solely to these two pieces of proposed legislation.

Most people agree that the legislation wasn't perfect and that some additional work was necessary to make the law effective. But the "sky is falling" reaction of the SOPA and PIPA opponents was remarkable, and further, these companies influenced millions of people, convincing them that their rights were being taken away. Now *that* is very ironic.

I contacted Gael MacGregor, a Los Angeles-based music supervisor, musician, songwriter, author, performer, and advocate for strong intellectual property rights for all content creators. Gael understands both sides of the argument pretty well—probably better than anyone. Here's what she had to say:

> The senators and congresspersons that support these bills are supporting the IDEA of intellectual property protection. They know little about the contents and/or implications of either bill, since many don't read the full legislation—they get summaries of a few pages, which may or may not be accurate or inclusive.

As for the RIAA, MPAA, and the U.S. Chamber of Commerce who are cheerleading these bills on? They don't care what we (songwriters/artists) think, want, or need. Their concern is the bottom line—how much money will they get as a result? And believe me, it's not the artist on the label who will reap the benefit. It's not the writer of the song who will be getting more money. It's not the author of the book who will have the lion's share of what might have been "lost" revenue due to piracy. It is the companies who own the publishing, the labels that own the sound recordings, etc.

Just because a few pennies trickle in for each view on YouTube, that doesn't mean that particular artist and/or publisher is going to be seeing the money for that view. Such monies go to the labels and publishers—and, as is the case with a lot of the PRO revenue, the "top performers" would likely be seeing a cut of all net revenues, not necessarily the artist or composer who created and/or performed the work embodied in any given video or whatever. It will all come back to who gets the money from the websites—and then where will the money go after collection? Will the artists and composers continue to be ripped off, or will they actually benefit from this legislation? I think it will be the former, and most composers and artists will be no better off than they were before.

If Gael's observations are correct, then we have two problems:

1. Artists, composers, and songwriters will be getting the short end of the stick (again).
2. The legislation as written (both SOPA and PIPA) is not adequate enough to solve the problem.

It will be important (for all of us) to see where this goes—and to maintain some level of optimism that the kinks will be worked out of the system, resulting in a win-win scenario. As far as the current situation goes, to use Gael's words:

I don't mean to make light of this, but I think a lot in the two bills lean toward a "throw the baby out with the bathwater" approach, which I don't believe will ultimately solve the problems anyway.

Well said, Gael.

New Trend or Valid Business Model? Fan Funding

Fan funding, also known as *crowdfunding*, is a very new trend that is gaining momentum particularly among musicians, bands, songwriters, and recording artists. With fan funding, you present your music or act to the public and ask them to pledge money in exchange for various incentives that might come later. So, you are no longer presenting your music to a label for consideration; you are presenting it to your fans.

Fan-funding sites actually act as host sites for your project's funding and will take some percentage of your "winnings" as payment for their services. The percentage varies from site to site, but on average you might expect 5 to 15 percent as their cut of the project.

Fan-funding sites are those such as:

- Kickstarter
- PledgeMusic
- RocketHub
- SellaBand
- Slicethepie
- ArtistShare

I could go on and on, so I will:

- Indiegogo.com
- Aucadia.com
- FeedTheMuse.net
- CashMusic.org
- Bandstocks.com

For a relatively new phenomenon, this list is fairly long, although it is not a complete and comprehensive list.

How Fan Funding Works

In theory, fan funding gives you the opportunity not only to finance your project, but to create more buzz while you're doing it. The process of fan funding empowers your ability as an artist to create strong ties to your audience—not to mention your *potential* audience.

Brian Meece, co-founder of RocketHub, believes a successful fan-funded project needs three important elements:

- The project
- The network
- The rewards

To be successful, the project should be an important one, such as your next EP or CD, and you should be passionate about it. Your network starts with your immediate family and friends—the people who support you now.

Next in your network are the relationships you've built up through your social media sites, and finally, the third part of your network is the people who don't know you at all yet. You theoretically will need all three parts of the network strategy to raise enough funds for your project.

Rewards are the goods and services you can provide in exchange for your project donations. You can construct various rewards based upon different price points of the donations. On the low end of the reward spectrum might be something like a special-issue T-shirt or a signed album. The next reward level up might include something like a large USB stick with all of your albums on it (including the one you're currently working on). At the high end of the spectrum, you might offer a day in the recording studio with you and/or an executive producer credit on your forthcoming album.

Most fan-funding sites start with a video explaining why you need the support (and financing) of your fans to begin (or complete) a project. Your video not only has to be convincing, but also has to have as much honesty and sincerity as you can possibly muster.

Is Fan Funding for Everyone?

Is fan funding for everyone, especially you? Maybe not—and as a matter of fact, there are those who are very opposed to the idea in the first place. Here are some of the most common objections to the practice:

- **You may be lying.** Or to put it more mildly, as the character Ben said in the series *Lost*, you could say, "I'm afraid I'm not being totally truthful with you." The reason you might not be telling the whole truth is that recording costs have taken a huge dive in recent decades, and recording costs are usually the largest cost of an album project. Funding requirements for a project in the old recording industry are not the same today, and funding for recording costs is usually the first item mentioned when a band or artist sets up their fan-funded web page.

- **You might experience loss of control.** With a fan-funded project, you are accountable to your contributors. In essence, they hold the key to whether the project becomes successful. Fan-funded marketing campaigns (because it really *is* marketing) are an all-or-nothing proposition. If you don't reach your monetary goal within the allotted time for the project, none of your contributors will have to pay, and you will receive no funds.

- **You might feel humiliated.** If you don't reach your goal, your fans may conclude that your music wasn't that good or you were just too ambitious. It is difficult to recover from this perception once your project fails. That's why you have to evaluate the positive and negative factors resulting from fan funding before you engage in it.

Fan funding might be a trendy, flash-in-the-pan concept that ultimately doesn't last, or it could be the future of the music business. There are some initial success stories out there and as many (actually, more) failures to look at. You have to determine whether it is right for you.

The One-Stop Digital Shop

Not surprisingly, there are websites and services designed to help songwriters and artists upload, package, and sell their music on the Internet. Many of them have similar attributes but with some small differences. All of them take advantage of social networking in their platforms. For bands, these sites are an integral part of their music-promotion efforts, and numerous sites offer services, tools, and dream fulfillment. For fans, these sites offer a platform for discovering and sharing new music.

It would take another book to list and describe every music platform—and perhaps someone is working on that book right now. So what I will do is take a close-up look at a few of them, starting with ReverbNation, a site that has been around for a while and seems to be doing well.

Close-Up: ReverbNation

Just a casual look at ReverbNation's homepage provides a fairly good description of what this site is about. Their tagline says "Home to Over 2.21 Million Musicians, Venues, Labels, and Industry Professionals." So you can immediately see that they are a band/artist platform as well as a music-discovery vehicle for fans. But when you look at the images and descriptions on the right side of the page, you can see they are offering a lot more.

- **For labels:** Work your roster—smarter tracking, promotion, and distribution.
- **For management:** Move the needle: Make an impact for your artists, a name for yourself.
- **For artists:** Conquer the Web: More fans, opportunities, gigs, stats, and money.
- **For venues:** Pack the house: Book the right bands, reach the right fans.
- **For fans:** Be a taskmaster: Find and share the best new music.

Each one of these categories is linked to another page customized with more detail, more tools, and more features. Features are divided into two main categories—free features and premium features.

ReverbNation for Artists

As an artist, you can opt for free features that are quite impressive. The profile page alone provides opportunities for playing and selling your music and videos. You can also choose to allow comments for interacting with your fans, direct connection to your Facebook page, displaying your blog (whether you write one here or import one you already have), and a whole lot more.

The free features for artists include:

- **Profile Page.** Upload, edit, and manage content across multiple platforms, all from your ReverbNation profile.
- **Web Buzz.** Read what people are saying about your band online.
- **Get on Facebook.** Band Profile is the #1 musician app on Facebook. Let your friends share songs and increase traffic to your page.
- **Detailed Statistics.** Track everything from number of fans to number of plays using easy-to-read stats.
- **Banners.** Free banners that link to your ReverbNation or Facebook profiles.
- **Blog.** Create a blog for your band or import one you already have.

- **Gig Finder.** Find gigs at venues that have booked artists similar to your band or venues similar to ones you've played.

- **Widgets.** Music players, show schedules, merch stores, and more—all available to paste anywhere you can think of.

- **Twitter Integration.** Update your tweople about all the things you do on ReverbNation automatically from your dashboard.

- **Reverb Store.** Free, on-demand store that sells your T-shirts, albums, downloads, and more, available right in your profile.

- **TunePacks.** The easiest way to send songs over email or IM.

Those are all *free* features, and I'd have to say that this looks like a pretty good deal.

When it comes to premium features, you can fork over various amounts of money for things such as:

- **Your Own Mobile App.** Promote your band with your own mobile app.

- **Digital Distribution.** Sell your music on iTunes, Amazon, and more. You keep the rights to your music.

- **FanReach Pro.** Customizable email templates with demographic targeting and robust tracking.

- **Reverb Press Kits.** Professional-grade digital press kit. Photos, bio, press clips, and a music player all in one.

- **Site Builder.** Build your band website using your ReverbNation content with just a few clicks.

- **Mega Song Storage.** Mega Song Storage increases your maximum song size to 100 MB from the standard 8 MB.

- **Pro Widgets.** Widgets, only better.

- **Promote It.** Get your music heard by new fans from around the world. Promote It delivers targeted ads for your band in the places that music lovers go to discover something new. Sites such as YouTube, Facebook, Pandora, MTV, and dozens more.

This is quite an array of features, whether free or paid. The thing to remember is this: Creating, managing, and updating an artist's page like this one on ReverbNation takes time. If you can't devote the necessary time to it, your effort may end up being futile.

ReverbNation for Labels and Managers

If you are a label or a manager, you can get these free features, some of which are the same as those for an artist and some that are specific for your needs. They include:

- **Central Artist-Management Page.** Upload, edit, and manage content from all of the bands on your roster, all from one central profile.

- **Detailed Statistics.** Track everything for all of your artists, from number of fans to number of plays, using easy-to-read stats, all available on one profile.

- **Exclusive Content.** Turn casual listeners into real fans by offering exclusive content from one or all of your artists, and get more information about who's listening.

- **FanReach Email.** Customizable email templates with demographic targeting and robust tracking.

- **Widgets.** Music samplers and show schedules of all of the artists on your roster, all available to paste anywhere you can think of.

Premium features for labels and managers include:

- **Your Own Mobile App.** Promote your band with your own mobile app.

- **Digital Distribution.** Sell your music on iTunes, Amazon, and more. You keep the rights to your music.

- **FanReach Pro.** Customizable email templates with demographic targeting and robust tracking.

- **Reverb Press Kits.** Professional-grade digital press kit. Photos, bio, press clips, and a music player all in one.

- **Site Builder.** Build your band website using your ReverbNation content with just a few clicks.

- **Mega Song Storage.** Mega Song Storage increases your maximum song size to 100 MB from the standard 8 MB.

- **Pro Widgets.** Widgets, only better.

- **Promote It.** Get your music heard by new fans from around the world. Promote It delivers targeted ads for your band in the places that music lovers go to discover something new. Sites such as YouTube, Facebook, Pandora, MTV, and dozens more.

I included these feature lists just to give you an idea about the depth and breadth of Reverb-Nation's offerings. I encourage you to go to their site and explore. Look at and listen to what other artists have done. Try to imagine whether this is the site for you, but also compare it to the myriad other artist sites before you jump in.

TuneCore

TuneCore is a slightly different concept that specializes in online music distribution. On this site you can get started with three easy steps:

1. Upload your music.
2. Upload your art.
3. Pick your stores.

For a fee, TuneCore will distribute your music to online music sites such as Amazon, eMusic, Spotify, and more. After signing up for and establishing an account, you upload your music and then your artwork. TuneCore supplies templates in the event that you don't have artwork ready to go.

You decide what price you want your album to be and target which stores you want to sell your music. TuneCore also provides sales reports for tracking sales, the profits of which you keep.

TuneCore now offers a Songwriter Service. TuneCore, as an organization, has been very concerned about the inequities of the "old" music business, especially if some of the unfair practices are seeping into the "new" music business. They will tell you, quite accurately, that anytime your music is downloaded or streamed, you are owed royalties. True, they may not amount to a lot, but if you don't claim the money, it is distributed to the major labels based on their market share.

Does this seem unfair? Correct, it is unfair. However, it's up to you to take the lead and do something about it. TuneCore's Songwriter Service allows you to register your songs and "they will do the rest." That's a hard deal to refuse.

If you are selling a lot of product through TuneCore, you will have more clout with record labels because those sales dollars demonstrate that you have numerous fans paying for your music. That, in and of itself, makes you more attractive to a label and possibly an old-fashioned record deal (if you're into that sort of thing).

Keep in mind that the Songwriter Service as well as TuneCore's distribution services are not free. You pay a monthly or annual fee for such services, although admittedly the prices are very reasonable.

Another "unadvertised" benefit of TuneCore is their email newsletter. Very often, it contains issues that are of direct importance to you in this new music business.

SoundCloud

SoundCloud is interesting because it has evolved right in front of my eyes, from one type of audio site to a full-fledged music-sharing site. Originally, SoundCloud provided a simple way of uploading audio to the Internet. People could provide links to the audio or embed the Sound-Cloud player directly into a web page.

What a Player

The SoundCloud player was unique from day one. It is displayed as an audio waveform that visually represents your audio. If nothing else, this makes it much more fun to click on.

However, there is more to the waveform than that. The waveform player lets you incorporate comments—timed comments, no less—so that listeners can provide feedback at a specific moment in the audio.

Social Studies

Somewhere along the line, SoundCloud became a social, sharing, showcasing type of site—not just a means for enabling audio playback. That's a pretty smart move, if you ask me. They started with the audio capability and added the social-networking features to it. Is it worthwhile to use SoundCloud to discover new music? Well, I tried doing just that today, and I discovered an amazingly cool track by a DJ/electronic/techno artist named Diplo featuring a vocal by Usher. The song is called "Climax," and it really rocks. So, based on just that one experience, I'd say it is worthwhile to use SoundCloud for discovering new music.

SoundCloud, like many other music/social applications, hooks you up directly with your Facebook account (and you actually log in using your Facebook username and password). Also, like many of these applications, you get the benefit of a mobile app for your iPhone or Android device. While some sites provide this only through their premium offering, SoundCloud gives it to you for free. Nice.

There's an App for That

Yes, indeed, SoundCloud offers hundreds of apps for mobile, desktop, and web to amplify your SoundCloud experience (their words, not mine). These apps are pretty cool overall, and there is even a T-Pain app, just in case you haven't had enough Auto-Tune yet. But there's more to this app, as they describe it:

> Get a jump start with over 50 song templates arranged from hundreds of professionally-designed beats, then grab a mic and sing, rap, or freestyle on 2 vocal tracks. Give your voice that distinctive T-Pain sound by cranking up The T-Pain Effect, or kick it down a notch for subtle pitch correction.

Apps are listed in categories of desktop, web, mobile, and other—and are further delineated by categories of Create & Record (such as the T-Pain app), Discover & Listen, and Share & Distribute. Be forewarned—these apps are not of the free or 99-cent variety; they seem to be priced much higher. You can even get Pro Tools 10 to integrate with your SoundCloud application, but at the steep price of $699.

I find SoundCloud to be an attractive option because it was originated by audio creators and then expanded to have the social-media marketing aspect on top of it. One thing I do not care for, however, is the need to log in through one's Facebook account. Facebook has made deals with several companies that have implemented this log-in, but I think it should be optional and not a requirement.

The Story of Nimbit   *To get additional insight into the direct-to-fan platform, I went to the powers-that-be at Nimbit. I have known about the company for a couple of reasons. First, they've been around for quite a while—since 2005, which in this business is similar to* *decades. Second, I ran into them when I spoke about my first book,* Make Your Music Video and Put It Online, *at the 2010 ASCAP Expo, where they were also exhibiting.*

Here is their story, in their words:

Founded by Phil Antoniades and Patrick Faucher, Nimbit is one of the leading direct-to-fan platforms for today's music business, used daily by thousands of artists and bands to connect with their fans online and give those fans easy ways to support them.

While some tools have been designed for professional marketers, Nimbit's mission is to be easy enough for the self-managed, D.I.Y. musician, but at the same time provide the powerful tools needed by managers and emerging labels.

"We take care of the hard stuff, so you can focus on your music and your fans," says Phil Antoniades, who continues "I take my inspiration from Charles Mingus who said 'Making the simple complicated is commonplace; making the complicated simple, awesomely simple, that's creativity.' That's where it's at for us and the core philosophy that guides our product decisions."

Nimbit fundamentally provides tools to grow and engage your fanbase, and sell music and merchandise online. That seems a little vague, so let's take a deep look at how we do that.

Key Features to the Nimbit platform:

- Sell digital and physical music, merchandise, and tickets from customizable storefronts for Facebook, Nimbitmusic.com, and your website. At the time of writing, Nimbit is currently the only storefront optimized for Facebook's timeline view.

- Expand your reach by integrating your Nimbit store with FanBridge, BandZoogle, PledgeMusic, Jango, Section101, and other partners.

- Nimbit will warehouse and ship all orders for physical goods.

- Sell your music on iTunes and stream your music on Spotify with free submission.

- Drive fans into your store using our Facebook Promo Tool with sharable Timeline and Ticker posts that can include video or a music player, personal messages, and a link to a free download.

- Fans can also easily share products on Facebook, Twitter, or email with deep links to your store.

- Fan comments/reviews made on your store appear throughout all your Nimbit storefronts as well as post to your fans' Facebook walls.

- Fans can provide additional support through Nimbit's in-cart tip jar for purchases and free downloads; on average 1-in-20 purchases receive a $7.80 tip.

- Offer products with Flexible pricing options: fixed price, name-your-price, or free to build your fanbase.

- Easily control it all with a centralized, streamlined dashboard that puts everything at your fingertips.

- Understand your fans and then better promote to them with detailed sales and fan activity reporting and grouping, and fan mapping to see and market to geographical hot-spots.

- Understand social activity with integrated Next Big Sound reporting to monitor your fans, followers, plays, views, and comments on Facebook, Twitter, YouTube, & Wikipedia.

- Get all the help you need with In-line help in the dashboard and connection with Nimbit's GetSatisfaction community.

So all in all, Nimbit is a complete direct-to-fan platform. Some success stories on the platform include Suzanne Vega who gave away free downloads using Nimbit, grew her Facebook fanbase from 7 to 70 thousand, and then later found that 61% of the individuals who accessed the free download later made a purchase. Another success was Ellis Paul, who set up a funding campaign to record and build excitement for his upcoming album and shattered his goal over $100K. Lesser known artists have also had some amazing results—for example, jazz singer Thisbe Vos asked fans to share a free track on Facebook in one post and received over 300 downloads and over 100 new fans.

The bottom line—if you are looking for an easy way to sell and promote your music and merchandise online, while simultaneously building your fanbase, we highly recommend that you take a look at Nimbit.

Author's note: After I completed my manuscript for this book, it was announced in July 2012 that Nimbit had been sold to PreSonus, a private acquisition that had actually concluded in April 2012 for an undisclosed sum. PreSonus is a maker of software and hardware products for audio production, including interfaces, mixers, and other accessories. The concept behind the merger is that users will now have an opportunity to buy an "end-to-end" solution for music production from creation to promotion to sales. Nimbit will continue operating in Massachusetts as a wholly owned subsidiary of PreSonus.

As an industry observer, I can only say that time will tell whether such a merger will prove valuable. I am somewhat skeptical of end-to-end solutions in an era where so many independent purchasing decisions can be made from thousands of product offerings to suit a creative person's specific needs. Perhaps this type of offering would work for someone who is building a studio setup almost from scratch and needs a mixer, some recording software, and a way to get a direct-to-fan (D2F) platform up and running—all at the same time.

Again, only time will tell whether this concept offers a truly competitive advantage.

One Size Digital Shop Doesn't Fit All

When you begin investigating one-stop digital shops, you'll find there is much more variety than I've indicated here. There are new ones cropping up every day, as well as older ones (CD Baby comes to mind) that have expanded their offerings to service the DIY songwriter.

You also will encounter sites that enable fans to download your music and sites that allow people to stream your music—or both. You need to decide what type fits you best.

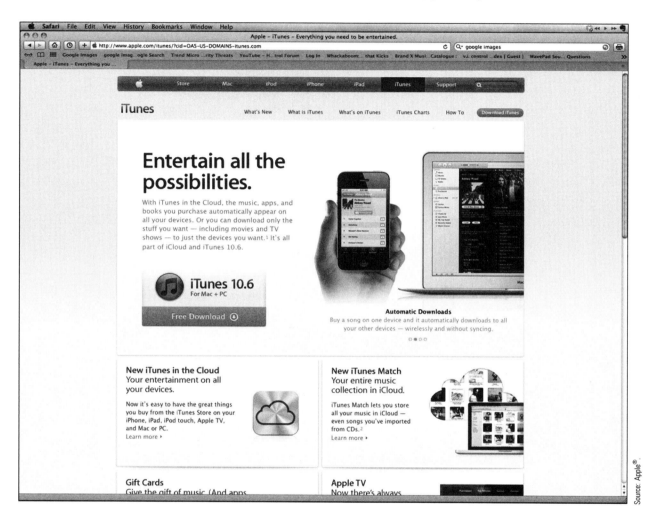

And without even investigating the latest trends, don't forget the recent ones, such as iTunes. As of today, iTunes is the largest source for digital music on the web, and with TuneCore or any number of other services, it's no longer difficult to get your music on iTunes, and hence, onto people's iPods, iPhones, iPads, and computers.

11 A License to Market Your Music (in a Music-Licensing Market)

Once upon a time, roughly in the 1960s, 1970s, 1980s, and 1990s, the Holy Grail of success in the music business was defined as a "Top 40" hit. The genres consisted of rock music, pop music, country, soul or R&B, dance, heavy metal, and so on. The 1970s and 1980s were heavily driven by the pop ballad. From Barry Manilow to Foreigner, artists were either self-contained acts who wrote their own music or artists who relied heavily upon submitted material—always seeking the elusive "single" to prop them up on the charts. The ballads consisted of love found or love lost, pulling at the heartstrings, providing a means for music listeners to identify with the pop culture of the time.

Like any good thing, too much of it can spell its demise. Top 40 became a victim of its own success, providing a means of filtering the musical wheat from the chaff, but at the same time, creating a playlist that was monotonous at best.

As time marched onward, pop ballads and other pop music were discovered, recorded, and launched through the vehicle of motion pictures, usually as tracks that played over the end credits. Sometimes these songs were within the body of the film itself, not only supporting the picture, but also helping to convey the emotion of it. On the extreme side of the spectrum, some motion pictures were completely music-driven. The examples that come to mind, in particular, are the Walt Disney film-musicals, from *The Little Mermaid* to *Beauty and the Beast* to *The Lion King*.

Music continued to infiltrate pop culture through TV shows. While this seems obvious to us today, it wasn't always so. There were no pop artists or rock bands helping to supply the soundtrack for *Leave It to Beaver, Jeopardy,* or *Dallas.*

Motion pictures and television shows have continued to benefit from the soundtrack, whether supplied by a composer, by popular music artists, or by a combination of both. The influence of music has expanded into the realms of advertising, product promotion, and even corporate identity. Music has also become an integral part of video games—not just *Pac-Man* boings and beeps, but full orchestral scores that create the excitement of an interactive title. Some video games incorporate music from an indie band that gets noticed because of their unique musical contribution to the video game.

This shift to music-driven media has coincided to some extent with the analog-to-digital transformation, although not exclusively. Still, someone had to step in and add some expertise to the choices being made about how media is best supported by music, and thus was born the *music supervisor.*

The Music Supervisor

A music supervisor is someone who chooses, manages, negotiates, and incorporates music into visual media. The music supervisor's responsibilities include both the creative and business sides of the process. Music supervisors can be employed by film studios, television studios, advertising agencies, cable or network production companies, or video game developers, or they might work independently on a freelance basis.

The significance of incorporating the right music into the right media has grown so large that the process has become an integral part of a media company's marketing strategy.

What a Music Supervisor Does

A music supervisor may work closely with a director, a producer, a creative director, music editors, or a combination of these to create a musical background consisting of original music from a composer or licensed music from an existing artist or band.

A music supervisor's responsibilities are not all fun and games by any stretch. They may need to manage budgets, acquire clearances, negotiate deals, secure artists or composers, and carry out any number of legal and financial aspects of licensing music for a production.

The role of a music supervisor in our present-day media culture cannot be overemphasized. One case in point is the importance of licensed music for the popular television show, *Grey's Anatomy*. This show relies heavily on songs from independent artists, songwriters, and bands and has been highly successful due to the efforts of music supervisor Alexandra Patsavas. She also demonstrated her music supervisory skills on dozens of other popular shows, including *Roswell, Boston Public, Criminal Minds, Without a Trace, Mad Men, The O.C., Private Practice,* and *Gossip Girl*. So influential are her successes that many indie artists and bands comprised soundtracks released on her own label, Chop Shop Records, including the soundtrack for the 2008 film, *Twilight*.

The careers of many independent artists were launched due to her talent and expertise, and many other music supervisors have become influential to media companies in the same way.

Why You Should Care about Licensing

It's not difficult to see the thread that flows through the ideas at the beginning of this chapter to now. There has been a seismic shift in the opportunities provided by old-school Top 40 radio—to the potential platforms of success made available by film, television, video game, and other media formats. No, radio has not disappeared, and in fact, many artists are being sustained by radio and new ones still being launched by it. But still, a person living in the 1970s or 1980s would have been declared insane if he insisted that many artists' careers in the future would be launched by completely different means than radio, let alone predicted that something called the Internet would change the world. Both ideas would have been grounds for permanent residence at the funny farm.

And so this change marks something more than a subtle difference in how music is exposed to the masses. It emphasizes a very specific marketing strategy that you must embrace and consider for your success—licensing your music.

You and perhaps the majority of the readers of this book are likely in one of these categories:

- Independent artist
- Unsigned artist
- Struggling songwriter
- Successful songwriter
- Composer for film or TV
- Composer for video games
- Musician wanting to "break in" to the business

Because this book deals with marketing your music, licensing your music *may* be an integral part of your success. I say "may" because it is just as possible that licensing your music may not become part of your strategy. One of the factors that comes into play is the type of music you are creating.

Musical Considerations for Licensing

Here are some things to keep in mind about the music itself when you consider licensing:

- Remember that sometimes less is more. You have to tell (and sell) a story in less than a minute at most, not the three-and-a-half minutes of typical pop songs.

- Cut to the chase—get to the main point with your lyrics as quickly as possible.

- Highlight a universal experience—love found, love lost, and so forth—and stay with that theme.

- After focusing on a theme, don't get too detailed or specific. "I love you" will be more adaptable to a scene than "I love Mildred." You get the idea.

- Make sure your track works with dialogue and doesn't swallow it up. This one is easier said than done. Even successfully licensed tracks sometimes violate this principle.

- Create a great song—the above factors don't mean that your song has to be any less strong than a memorable hit. The emotional impact must be there.

Increasing Your Odds

If you want to increase your odds of placing your music, remember to:

- Do your homework. Watch television. Discover which show is incorporating what kind of music.

- Identify which music supervisors work with what shows. Music supervisors hate it when you call up and ask, "So, what are you working on?" (See "Researching Music Needs for Film and Television" later in this chapter.)

Understanding the Business

Music licensing can be a complex topic. Different types of licenses are required, depending on the type of deal that is negotiated. These were mentioned in Chapter 10, but they bear mentioning again because of their importance.

Licensing for Audio/Visual Works

- **Synchronization rights.** The right to use the music in sync with the visual element in a film, television program, commercial, and so on. This right is obtained from the publisher or the songwriter if there is no publisher involved. This right has to do with the song itself.

- **Master use right.** The right to use the actual master recording. The grant to use the sound recording comes from the record label, the music library, or the songwriter, depending on who owns the actual copyright.

- **Performing right.** Every time a song is broadcast, it constitutes a public performance. The royalties from public performance are distributed to publishers and songwriters from the PROs (performance rights organizations), such as ASCAP, BMI, and SESAC.

It is the first two rights mentioned here—synchronization and master use—that come into play when negotiating a license. The performing right is "automatic" in that performance royalties are paid automatically by the PRO to which the publisher and songwriter belong.

Getting Paid

Licensing payments are all over the map, so to speak. They can vary widely, especially based upon the relative success or importance of the artist or songwriter. Table 11.1 provides some rough ballpark estimates.

Table 11.1 Licensing Fees

Type of Usage	Description	Amount Paid
Low-end television usage	Incidental music playing in the background, sometimes called source music.	Free (for exposure) to $2,000 for five-year use in television program. Usage in film could be roughly $10,000.
Popular song	Used as a theme song.	$50,000 to $75,000 in a film.
TV commercial	Original song, per year.	$25,000 to $500,000. A well-known song can *typically* command $75,000 to $200,000 per year.

Note that these amounts are what you might find in an ideal situation, carefully negotiated by you or, better yet, someone on your behalf (such as a lawyer). Very often, unfortunately, licensors will present the "free, for exposure" option, which you should avoid unless you are absolutely desperate.

Music-Licensing Websites

Recently, there has been a proliferation of music-licensing websites. This is no coincidence. Many people have seen (or foreseen) the opportunities made available by music licensing and have constructed services, usually in the form of websites, to act as a go-between type of agent. Songwriters and artists can upload their music to such a site, and those needing music can license it. The website usually takes a cut of the action. Be careful, however, of the conditions being offered. Sometimes these sites are known as "pay-to-play," meaning that in addition to providing your music, you are asked to pay a fee. Avoid these sites if at all possible.

Listing these types of websites would take pages and pages (which would do wonders for this book's page count but wouldn't necessarily be of help to you). I decided not to list any of them here because they vary widely in their capabilities not only to help you, but also to keep your interests at heart. Use Google to search them out, and by all means read the reviews about these sites before you decide to sign up for their services.

You may also want to check out Music Library Report (www.musiclibraryreport.com), which reviews music libraries as reported by those who use them. Music libraries that ask for your music submissions are acting as licensing agents (building up their catalog from music from songwriters and composers such as you) and then licensing that music to their clients (production companies, broadcasters, website developers, and so on).

Reaching a Music Supervisor Directly

This is the most elusive, evasive, confounding part of the music-supervisor equation. I call it a Catch 23—which is like a Catch 22, only worse.

As I mentioned previously, music supervisors don't want to be bombarded by phone calls from artists and songwriters. This is because they *already are* bombarded by phone calls from artists and songwriters. What's worse for the supervisor is when they are confronted with song sellers who have no idea what the supervisor is looking for, working on, or in need of. If you can be resourceful enough to figure this out *before* you call, and you *only* call a supervisor when you have music that is highly appropriate, then good for you.

If you *can't* figure out these important pieces of the puzzle, you could be out of luck. It's not an easy task, and hence why I consider it a Catch 23.

Is it a good idea to even *try* to go directly to a music supervisor? I asked this question of Shawn Clement, a successful composer for film, television, and video games who deals with music supervisors a great deal. Here's what he had to say to the question, "Should artists send their material to music supervisors as their main vehicle to place music?"

> If they're a songwriter or songwriter/artist, then yes, that should be one of their main vehicles; because especially with video games, such as these sports games or racing games, if they hear your music over and over and like it, that can break your band, and that's really key. It's

better than radio, because who listens to radio anymore? Even when you do listen to radio, most of it is talk radio or classic rock radio, and they're going to play the same songs over and over every hour.

So, yes, go to music supervisors, but they're mostly working on the "gig-of-the-day." So you want to research as much as you can about what they're doing and find out what shows they're working on now and only send them stuff that relates to what they're working on. Even if you send them a bunch of stuff blindly and they think that it's cool, they'll think, "Okay, I'll call him when I need to." But then, at that point, it's done—they'll file it away because they're focusing on the gig *today*. So, for example, if you know they're working on *True Blood*, you send them something and say, "Hey, I think this is perfect for what you're working on," and that way, they're going to pay attention.

Read additional insights provided by Shawn in the interviews section of Chapter 14, "Learning from the Experience of Others."

Researching Music Needs for Film and Television

Shawn Clement provided some clues and helpful resources for aiding your research on film and television music-production needs.

- Check out IMDb (www.imdb.com). You can look into what film and television projects are in production or are about to be in production. Find out who's who and what's what, and then make contact. Make sure you know what they might need *before* you start to dial—and sign up for a "pro" membership (at about $100/year).

- You can also subscribe to a production newsletter called *Below the Line* at www.findfilmwork.com. A monthly subscription for about $7 to $10 will keep you abreast of media-production listings from all over the world.

- Production Weekly (www.productionweekly.com) provides the entertainment industry with a comprehensive breakdown of projects in pre-production, preparation, and active development for film and television, albeit at a much higher price tag of around $400 per year.

Be True to Your School

Lastly, it is important to be true to yourself, musically speaking. Don't try to contrive some music that you think will work for some project, because it will sound, well...contrived. Whatever and whoever you are as an artist is of utmost importance. If you stay focused on that, there may very well be a licensing opportunity waiting for you somewhere down the line.

Oh, I almost forgot—never get discouraged. Licensing is a tough, competitive business. Hopefully, you will see signs of progress as you work on your career, even if you sometimes encounter signs like this that are not very encouraging:

**We do not need any new music at this time.
Unsolicited submissions will not be accepted.**

Just keep moving forward.

12 The Music Library Phenomenon

usic from a music library may be known as production music, stock music, or library music. A music library is not the type of library you would find on a university campus or in Washington D.C. You would very likely find it, however, in Hollywood, California.

Production or library music is pre-recorded, is owned by the music library or production company, and is licensed to clients for use in film, radio, television, web, and other media. Library music is frequently used for underscore in television shows, independent films, and television commercials, and is very often an instrumental composition—although recent trends in music licensing from libraries or directly from independent artists has included vocal arrangements, typical of a contemporary rock or pop band.

A Brief History of Production Music

Production music used to imply music that was bland, sterile, uninteresting, devoid of emotion, blasé, boring, or otherwise uninteresting. That's because production music *was* bland, sterile, uninteresting, devoid of emotion, blasé, boring, or otherwise uninteresting.

Times have changed. The same technologies that have lowered the bar to entry in music composition for the masses have influenced the music library business as well. Sure, on the low end there are tracks that may sound amateurish, because they are written and recorded by, well... amateurs. But in the hands of professional composers who know what they're doing, current music technology can provide the tools for one composer to sound like an orchestra—and very frequently, this is the case.

Somewhere around the 1990s, music production libraries used their own marketing messages to convey that their music was superior to the boring, blasé music of the production libraries of old. Soon, many libraries began to make the same claim, until eventually all music libraries were making the same claim. Now it is once again difficult to differentiate some libraries from others, because either they're all great (and many actually are) or they are simply making the same claim as to how great they are.

Still, the main message is clear—obtaining music from a production music library doesn't mean that the music is inferior. In many cases, the music can be quite impressive.

Today's Music Library Landscape

You might find it hard to believe that music libraries have proliferated to the point where they've become commoditized. The landscape is filled with so many competing music libraries that the market is almost saturated with them. As I mentioned previously, some are good, some not so good, and some are great—but nevertheless, the sheer quantity of music libraries has made differentiation between them a more difficult task to achieve. Music libraries may be small, independent companies, or they may be part of larger corporations such as Universal Music or Warner Brothers, or they may evolve from the former to the latter. They may vary in catalog sizes of a few hundred to thousands of musical compositions.

Competition between music libraries has become fierce along with their proliferation in numbers. This has made them a double-edged sword—they provide a lot of musical choice to clients, but (as with most business models) this has driven licensing fees downward.

History, in a sense, is repeating itself. In Chapter 2, I discussed how individual songwriters can contribute to the concept of "music is free." Now, in the case of the libraries, the music may not be offered for free per se, but competitiveness with other libraries encourages some to offer license fees for pennies on the dollar or to license entire music collections for prices that used to apply to one or two songs. And around and around we go.

Still, this hasn't stopped new music libraries from popping up every day, nor has it (or should it) prevent you from looking at music libraries as an additional revenue source.

The Major Music Libraries

This is where I have to state once again not to send in cards and letters (or should I say emails and text messages?) complaining that I left someone's company name out of a particular list. To list every music library in existence would take another book (which is a cliché meaning that it would take too much time and trouble). Nevertheless, I will list some of the better-known music libraries, most of which are members of the PMA (Production Music Association). It should be of some significance that the PMA doesn't mind using the word "Production" in their name, as I previously alluded to the historical aversion to the concept of "production" music.

The Production Music Association (PMA)

The PMA mission statement includes the following:

> The Production Music Association ("PMA") brings together publishers and composers of production music to promote and protect the interests and rights of our community. The PMA is a non-profit, volunteer organization currently comprising 445 member companies, including major-label publishers and national independents, and is providing crucial leadership to protect the value of our work and create an even better future for our community.

The PMA supports high values in music production as well as high concepts in the valuation of music itself. A meeting in February 2012 was entitled "What's the Value of Music"—many of the concepts I discuss in this book comprised the topics discussed in that meeting.

PMA Member Companies

Some of the PMA companies include:

- 5 Alarm Music
- 615 Music
- APM
- Immediate Music
- Killer Tracks
- Manhattan Production Music
- Megatrax Production Music
- Music Box
- Non-Stop Production Music
- Omni Music
- Riptide Music
- Universal Publishing Production Music
- Videohelper
- X-Ray Dog Music

There are many, many more music library companies than this. To see a listing (and this is a listing of *only* PMA companies), visit www.pmamusic.com.

Libraries within Libraries

Just as there are genres within genres (as you will see in the next section), there are sometimes libraries within libraries. Some libraries have created alliances and/or distribution deals that pool their resources so that music licensees can find what they want—fast. There also may be a need for a library to expand its catalog into areas that are popular but not the library's specialty, such as indie music. Indeed, the popularity of independent artists and bands placing songs with libraries (and hence, film or TV shows) has grown rapidly in the past few years, and it hasn't slowed down yet.

Music libraries with such arrangements make split deals amongst themselves to share in the profits, but the artist or songwriter simply benefits from the deal and doesn't lose any revenue in the process.

Understanding the Music of Production Libraries

How do you write a piece of music for film or television if you haven't seen the visual element to which you're scoring? You write, or pre-write the music, keeping the visual aesthetic in mind. Because of the necessity of writing to picture-without-picture, a wide variety of musical genres must be addressed to accompany a multitude of possibilities.

Music Genres

As a songwriter or composer, you may have certain strengths or weaknesses, and as a matter of fact, you *should* (otherwise, you don't have a *focus*). So write to your strengths, and if you happen to be somewhat versatile, then that's all the better.

Here are just *some* of the musical genres that comprise production library music catalogs:

- Ambient
- Bluegrass
- Blues
- Breakbeat
- Children's music
- Chill out
- Classical
- Club
- Comedy
- Christian
- Country
- Dance
- Disco
- Drums 'n bass
- Dubstep
- Electronic/electronica

- Folk
- Funk
- Gospel
- Grunge
- Heavy metal
- Hip-hop
- House
- Jazz
- Latin
- New age
- Period music
- Pop (instrumental)
- Pop (vocal)
- Punk
- Rap (vocal)
- Rap (underscore)
- Rave
- Reggae
- Rhythm and blues
- Rock (mainstream)
- Rock (alternative, indie)
- Ska
- Soul
- Techno
- Trance
- Trip-hop
- Urban
- World
- World pop

Source: Billboard.com.

Aside from these genres, there are many possible subgenres. For example, under the category of heavy metal, you could conceivably break it down further into:

- Death metal
- Thrash metal
- Black metal
- Power metal
- Progressive metal
- Gothic metal
- Doom metal
- Alternative metal
- Glam metal (an oxymoron?)
- Industrial metal
- Sludge metal
- Stoner metal

- Speed metal

- Christian metal (*has* to be an oxymoron)

Although a music library may not be this detailed in its breakdown of genres, you will often see a very specific request for music go out from a music library that contains this much detail and more. For example, consider this actual request for a music library submission, posted on the Film Music Network's job-listing board:

> Nashville publisher working on new drag-race reality show is immediately seeking high-energy, rock, and any new and current style music that would go with energy of racing, a crowd, enthusiastic drivers, anticipation of race outcome, winner of race. Energizing vocals in the music. Seeking bumpers (60–90 seconds) and whole songs.

The description of high-energy rock and the types of emotions are very specific, but the phrase "any current style of music" could keep you busy guessing for quite a while.

If you can write that type of music, consider this request, found in another posting:

> Music library is seeking authentic dubstep tracks for several production company clients. Must be instrumental, containing no vocals. Looking for that authentic dubstep sound with drops, wobble bass, stutters and glitches.

These are typical, yet understated examples of the amount of detail I've seen compared to others from time to time. The descriptions can be head-spinning, mind-boggling, and otherwise confusing. Admittedly, requests from music libraries are often better articulated than those that are directly from film or video production companies. The lack of music knowledge in production companies often shows, with requests that don't really give the songwriter/composer enough to go on.

Music Collections or Series

Music libraries usually organize their catalogs into groups, and while organizing the music by genre is typical, there are other methods as well. For example, trailer music is not a genre, per se, but it is a specific type of music. So, one of the music library's collections might very well be trailer music, which is a typical application for the music. Trailer music itself can have a subcategory such as beds, drones, hits, crashes, and splashes—or all together might be marketed as a trailer "toolkit."

In addition, libraries can be subcategorized by mood. So, considering all of the possibilities, you might find listings that are segmented by application, mood, or genre, such as:

- Sports music

- Crime drama

- Thriller/suspense

- Uplifting
- Heroic
- Tension
- Romance
- Technology/science
- Playful
- Competitive
- Light tension
- Orchestral underscore
- Commercials
- Contemporary
- Promos (:15, :30, :60)
- Cinematic underscore

Licensing Fees and Performance Royalties

Organization of libraries by groups usually goes beyond simple categorization. Very often, these collections might belong to a particular CD or CD collection that is covered by a blanket license. In these cases, the licensee, which might be a radio station, television station, or production company, pays a blanket fee for the use of that CD for a specified amount of time (usually yearly). This is as opposed to licensing individual songs or tracks from the library as a whole. Either way, you, as the songwriter, are entitled to collect royalties. Depending on the deal you have, you may share in the upfront licensing fees with the music library or just your performance royalties on the back end (from whichever performing rights organization, or PRO, you belong to), or a combination of both. In any and all cases, you are relying on the honesty and accurate bookkeeping of the library, which is required to submit detailed cue sheets to the performing rights association so that you can keep those checks coming in.

To Title or Retitle, That Is the Question

One of the more controversial issues surrounding library deals is that of retitling. Some time ago, someone thought it would be nice to acquire material that already belonged to another library or publishing company. Naturally, you're not supposed to be able to do this—a copyright is a copyright, right? Well, copyrights are registered by their titles, and that's how they are cataloged by publishing companies and PROs. But what if the track or song had a completely different name? In other words, what if it was the same music but had a different name? Wouldn't that be a way of having your material in more than one library at a time?

In a word, yes.

Sallee's Music Library					
Catalog No.	Cut No.	Title	Genre	TRT	PRO
SA006151	3	Falling in Love	Romance	2:15	ASCAP

Johnny's Music Library					
Catalog No.	Cut No.	Title	Genre	TRT	PRO
JO139482	9	Love Falling	Romance	2:15	ASCAP

There are some advantages and disadvantages to this idea, and it can be complicated, so I will talk about it in simplified terms.

As a music creator, retitling provides more freedom to market your music. You can place your tracks with more than one library, or even a dozen libraries. This, in turn, increases your odds of getting your music placed in a show or production. You can use your music again anywhere, for that matter—not just in other music libraries. Your deal with a library under this type of arrangement is *non-exclusive,* by default. You cannot use the retitling method if you have an exclusive arrangement with one music library.

As a music library, you have access to a larger pool of music, even if you discover and want to sign tracks that a songwriter has placed (under a non-exclusive agreement) with another library.

Sounds good, doesn't it?

Well, not so fast. In recent years, some music libraries and publishers have grown uneasy with this type of deal. It stems from the fact that if there is a conflict with a licensee (such as a production company) that wants to use a track and discovers duplicate versions from different sources, someone is going to be unhappy. Which company owns the rights to the track? Who gets paid? And, even worse, it is technically a violation of copyright to copyright a title more than once, even if it is from the same content creator.

It is rumored that some production companies have started to back off from using tracks unless they are exclusively licensed to the music library or publishing company. I have personally seen this happen with some of the companies I do business with. This is unfortunate, because for the songwriter/artist, the distinct advantage of being able to hold on to your publishing rights is a small tree in a forest of disadvantages experienced by content creators everywhere. As one person once put it, if I'm selling Coke, I want to be able to have it in as many vending machines as possible.

For now, the future of Cokes by a different name has an uncertain vending-machine future.

Producing Music for Production Libraries

In the days of old, when production music had a bad name, the music may have been recorded in a large recording facility, or it may have originated from a small project studio. In either case, if the music *itself* was bad, the production values didn't really matter. Bad music is bad music. Bad production music is *really* bad music.

As time marched forward, the technology and tools accessible to songwriters and composers improved at a rapid clip, until eventually it almost became difficult to tell the difference between a studio recording and a home-based workstation recording. (Notice that I said *almost*.) Further, with ever-shrinking budgets (or no budgets whatsoever), the advantages to project-studio recording became more and more apparent (not to mention, *necessary*).

Today's music libraries have a very large quantity of music that has originated from project studios. But the same concepts of old still apply—bad music is bad music, and a bad recording is a bad recording. The type of music that will stand up in a music-library setting must be of the highest caliber, the best quality, and the most current production standards. Anything less will be (and should be) rejected. You need to keep this in mind if you are thinking of any get-rich-quick-with-a-music-library schemes.

Additionally, some music libraries have a strong preference for studio recordings, as opposed to home-baked, sample-library-based MIDI tracks. Some libraries are leaning heavily in favor of studio recordings, depending on the genre of music, of course. At the end of the day, it all is really a matter of quality. In the right hands, a DAW (digital audio workstation) can produce a fairly convincing orchestral track for use in a trailer or TV show. A recording of an indie band might be better served by using a studio, complete with isolation booths, miked amps (as opposed to direct-in recording), and the capability to record full drum kits, including overhead mics.

The music library of today has become highly competitive with other libraries *and* highly competitive amongst the composers who write for them. Consider this: Wouldn't it be more difficult in a competitive market such as this if *your* competition were the likes of say, a Hans Zimmer or a Danny Elfman? Well, guess what. You know what I'm getting at, don't you? They and dozens and dozens of top-name, A-list composers and songwriters are submitting material to today's music libraries. Granted, Hans is not shopping around, trying to get noticed. He has specific deals with a company or two, often for material that never made it into the movie. He simply had it sitting on a shelf somewhere, gathering dust. Now he has it on another shelf somewhere, gathering money.

But don't let this discourage you. If you feel you have a knack for pre-writing music for a visual scene, whether television, film, or commercial, then by all means, go ahead and do so. Just make sure you study the business landscape as well as constantly improve your songwriting craft.

Submitting Material to a Music Production Library

If you haven't already placed material with a library, then it might be hard to know how your music stacks up with the rest of the competition. The best way to find out, if you're just starting out, is to go ahead and give it a shot (after completing this book, naturally).

The PMA music libraries that I listed in the beginning of this chapter might be shooting too high, at least at first. You might consider targeting some of the smaller independent libraries. Your old friend Mr. Google can help, as usual. Search out the libraries and find their websites. See what their submission policies are and listen to the sample music they have on their sites. If they have CD samplers of their library that they're willing to send out, get a hold of them. Study them and share them with your band or any co-writers, if you have them.

In an ideal world, it would be nice to find out what specific needs a music library might have for their catalog. Perhaps they're up to their ears (pardon the pun) in country music but need some electronic music tracks. Maybe they have all the instrumentals they need right now and are looking for the next "undiscovered" indie act. Maybe, maybe, and maybe. The reason I said "in an ideal world" at the beginning of this paragraph is because it can be very difficult to find out what a library's needs are at a given point, depending on your relationship with them. You see, just like music supervisors, production library owners are swamped with emails, requests, phone calls, and text messages. And that's just from their spouses! If you consider all the different companies, partners, licensees, licensors, and others they have to communicate with, you can see how busy they really are (next to music supervisors, that is).

13 How to Keep Up with "the Change"

I have made comments throughout this book about the rapidly changing landscape of the music industry. The initial driver of this transformation may have been the transition from the analog to digital world. But it has gone beyond that now, this time propelled by further changes within the digital world, such as new technologies, new models for music commerce, and hundreds of websites that either support or create new ways of looking at how music is made. Once again, the Chinese curse "May you live in interesting times" comes to mind.

Your role as a DIY artist/musician is to ensure that you are aware of and embrace these changes. You may decide that the whole new music industry and everything that goes along with it is not for you. That's fine—but you still need to be aware of the changes so that you can make wise decisions.

So, given this rapidly changing landscape, how do you keep up with it all?

Music News on the Web

Some of the online sites for music news are mostly based on the worlds of Music 1.0. One example of this is Billboard.biz. Although they do publish some news about changes in the digital-music domain, they still have their roots—and most of the articles are in—the traditional music business.

Some sites are music blogs that also serve as a marketing tool for their owners. One example of this is arielpublicity.com—which is music news for DIY artists such as the ones she may (or may not) represent in her PR business. There is nothing at all wrong with this approach. As a matter of fact, this is exactly one of the methods I've been promoting in this book—encouraging you to create and manage a blog that promotes you or your band. A blog is, after all, a marketing and promotional tool.

Still another type of site is the kind that simply puts valuable digital music news out on the web for your consumption. Here you might find more objectivity about the business. Then again, that depends on what side of the business you are on.

I encourage you to check out these sites—you might be surprised by the amount of useful knowledge you can gain from someone else's experiences.

Some of the Key Players

In no particular order, some of the key players are:

- **Hypebot.com.** Their tagline says it all: "music. technology. the new music business." Bruce Houghton gathers some of the best posts from the web and aggregates them here. Some of these great articles are by Houghton himself. I highly recommend this site.

- **MusicThinkTank.com (managed by Hypebot).** A great site not only for gaining an understanding of the new music business; Music Think Tank also offers plenty of valuable tips on how to navigate through the creative process.

- **Billboard.biz.** Billboard's online publication has one foot in the past and one foot in the present music industries. (Okay, maybe a foot-and-a-half in the past.)

- **DigitalMusicNews.com.** Go to digitalmusicnews.com and sign up for their Daily Snapshot. Your inbox will receive valuable information every day on the new music industry, from technologies to legalities.

- **www.topix.com/business/online-music.** If you go to the precise URL listed here, you get the news from Topix on the music biz, aggregated from more than 450,000 sources. It's an interesting mix, although their algorithm might occasionally produce an article about a cement mixer rather than a Mackie mixer.

- **CreateDigitalMusic.com.** A blog targeted toward music creators and their arsenal of gear. Good reading.

- **Buzzsonic.com.** Buzzsonic is an aggregator of music, tech, and social media news.

- **MusicWeek.com.** As is the case with Billboard.net, Music Week is slanted toward the landscape of traditional music, but with some digital delights included on the side.

- **DigitalMusicTrends.com.** This is a great podcast on digital music and music tech startups. You can access the audio right on their website, and there are lots of interesting topics.

- **Mi2n.com (Music Industry News Network).** This site has a little of everything, and a lot of it. It's packed with articles, news, stories, and links on a variety of topics. Warning: If you're over 40 years of age, go find your reading glasses—the print is a bit small.

- **arielpublicity.com/category/blog.** Ariel's blog has some useful tips, especially for newcomers. She was one of the first people to catch on to the Music 2.0/3.0 phenomenon, and she uses her knowledge to the utmost while marketing her PR clients in the music biz as well as using social media to promote music for the general good of music lovers. She's very bright, articulate, and knowledgeable.

- **digitalaudioinsider.blogspot.com.** This is a great site and one of the most cutting-edge resources for current digital music information. They also cut right to the chase, and they're very real, such as in their informative articles on the royalties (or lack thereof) that music sites pay.

- www.artistshousemusic.org. Not only do they have articles on marketing and merchandising for your music, they have just about every subject under the sun. You can find a tremendous number of videos from industry experts. Highly recommended.

- Pro-music.org. If you comb through this site, you might pick up a few good nuggets of information, but it's not very well organized and has a slight identity crisis. (What does it want to be when it grows up?) Still, it's worthwhile to check out.

- EchoLouder.com. Although this site is more like an ongoing editorial from owner Bruce Warila, the subjects he tackles—as well as his perspective on them—make it very well worth your time. Bruce co-launched Music Think Tank (mentioned at the beginning of this list) and helped make it a success. Check out echolouder.com.

The Best of the Best: The Dean's List

In just about every endeavor, there are things that are *good* and things that are *great*, (which is many notches above good). There are sports announcers, and then there is Vin Scully. There are singers; then there is Frank Sinatra. There are innovative CEOs; then there is Steve Jobs. You probably get the picture.

To learn about music on the web, technology, and copyright issues, there is nothing better than the greatest of all—*The Dean's List*. As a matter of fact, this email newsletter is subtitled "Music, Copyright and New Technology in the News—From a Creator's Perspective." That pretty much sums it up, and the content that Dean Kay puts together from a variety of sources is invaluable—and it is fresh every single day.

Dean Kay is a songwriter and businessman who has been plugging away at it for a long time. He wrote the song made famous by Frank Sinatra, "That's Life." He has worked with Elton John, Don Williams, Ricky Skaggs, and many others. He has been a member of the board of directors at ASCAP since 1989 and heads up its New Technologies Committee. He knows the music business—both old and new.

Aside from gathering news from a variety of excellent sources, the content is true to the newsletter's subtitle—music, copyright, and new technology. It is at this very intersection that all of the changes—big and small—are taking place in our digital age. After reading *The Dean's List*, you'll feel a whole lot smarter.

So if you want to keep up with "the change" (and I assume you do), I strongly urge you to subscribe to *The Dean's List*. To do so, send an email to deankay1@deankay.com and include your name, your affiliation or profession, and your email address. There is no charge to get the daily dose of *The Dean's List*.

Trade Magazines

Here's the rub: Just about any trade magazine you would want to receive is available online or by email. The list in this chapter has almost all of the resources you would need (as far as news sources go). There are still print editions of *Billboard* magazine, *Variety*, *The Hollywood Reporter*, and more—but they're available online as well.

Networking

I'm fairly certain you've heard the word *networking* bandied about. It is probably one of the most important activities you need to do, and it requires highly elusive skills—elusive because there is no specific manual for how you engage in networking successfully. One thing that comes close, however, is a book by music-industry veteran Dan Kimpel (www.dankimpel.com) called *Networking Strategies for the New Music Business* (Course Technology PTR, 2005). This is a great resource for self-assessment and a guide to making your personal strengths and relationships work for you in the music business. Dan has conducted tons of interviews with music-industry professionals and is often a speaker at music-industry events. If you want to know a lot about networking, don't ask me—ask Dan Kimpel (but start by reading his book).

Industry Conferences and Events

The cool thing about conferences and seminars is that they are *current*. It would be difficult (if not impossible) to go to a music-industry conference to hear speakers discuss the advantages of cassette tapes over eight-track tapes. You will hear about the latest and greatest technologies, however, as well as pointers on how to be successful in this ever-changing business.

Share and Share Alike?

At the beginning of Chapter 10, I posed these two questions:

Do people want to *own* their music?

Or...

Do people simply want *access* to their music?

One final thought I like to contemplate is this:

Do people really want to share their music?

Many of the current musical trends are modeled around the idea that discovering new music is best accomplished by consumers sharing their music choices through playlists or a great number of other music-discovery tools and websites. With more and more sites partnering with Facebook as a means of logging into *their* site, your music choices can be immediately seen by others in your personal network, which may raise your red privacy flag (or not).

So I sometimes wonder if everyone is really on the music-sharing bandwagon. If there is only a small minority of music lovers who discover music this way, then the music-sharing/discovery idea really puts a dent in many of the concepts that comprise the backbone of today's music websites.

I pose the question as something to ponder. Because very often, a strong current can develop from an idea that is not time-tested and can possibly take the river in a direction that is unforeseen and undesirable. This, once again, speaks to the advantage of combining both traditional marketing and the digital, Internet-driven marketing of the new music business. Doing so helps to prevent having all of your musical eggs in one electronic basket.

Why do I bring this question up *here*, in a chapter entitled "How to Keep Up with 'the Change'"?

The reason is simple: Do everything you can to keep current on music-industry events, news, and trends. But when you do so, also keep a keen focus on asking yourself important (or even controversial) questions: Is this approach for me? Will this trend last? Does picking up and using the telephone best email or other electronic communication in this case? Am I doing this because I want to be seen with the "in crowd," or is this approach really the best way to achieve my goals?

Ask questions. Always have a dose of healthy skepticism. You very well could end up being a trendsetter rather than a crowd follower.

14 Learning from the Experience of Others

There are experts in every field. How they got to be experts varies from person to person, company to company, and industry to industry. Experts in the business of music are not necessarily the people who studied the most or practiced the most (although these things can never hurt). In the music business, experience often seems to be the best teacher. Most experts have been to the school of hard knocks—where they graduated with honors and received their diplomas (but not necessarily ones that you can frame and hang on a wall). These are the people to look to when you're searching for a path to follow. And speaking of paths, you'll often find that no two successful songwriters, composers, or players followed the same exact path to get to the top of the mountain. Indeed, someone once said, "There are many paths to the top of the mountain" (although he may have been referring to religion and not hip-hop music).

Experience as the best teacher was as true in the old music business as it is in today's music business—although today, everything is more complex, there are more options or variables, and most of all, there are completely unexpected ways in which some acts rise to the top of public attention and adoration.

The Music Business—Today and Tomorrow

I have brought up many ideas and viewpoints about the music business of old, the music business of the present, and even some references to the music business of the future. The risk in doing so is that my opinion is just that—my opinion.

So, in the interest of being fair, balanced, and more popular with the contacts in my personal network (no, not really—well, yes, really), I decided to solicit some viewpoints from other music-industry professionals.

I think you will find these interviews very interesting. Sometimes the opinions are very similar, and at others they are very different. This demonstrates, if nothing else, how much we are still in the midst of violent, game-changing, evolutionary change.

The questions I asked were based on some general issues and trends that emerged as I wrote this book. The bulk of the questions were the same for each interviewee, but some questions varied according to the interviewee's background and expertise. Not every person answered every question, and some may have chosen to skip a few. But even without these particular differences, there is diversity in how the questions were answered—both in substance and in style.

And so, without further ado, let's see what other music-industry pros have to say.

The Interviews

You probably know how difficult it can be to get the attention of music-industry professionals when it comes to listening to your music or even to speaking with you about your career highs and lows. The same goes for getting music-industry pros to take a few minutes out of their busy schedule to answer some interview questions. About 80 percent of those I contacted were more than willing to participate, and about 10 percent of them were ultimately unable to carve out time in their schedules to actually respond to the questions. Still, those are pretty good averages.

You'll notice that there are a few representatives from ASCAP in these interviews but no one from BMI or SESAC. This was simply due to those averages I mentioned above—at the end of the day, representatives from those companies would not or could not respond.

You will notice an interesting cross-section of interviewees—artists, songwriters, composers, music supervisors, publicists, promoters, journalists, publishers, record-industry executives, music licensors, licensees, and heads of music-industry groups or associations. Although this may not represent everyone in the business, it is still a respectable "focus group."

It was a joy to see what each respondent said (or didn't say), how his viewpoint might be skewed by his position (or not), and ultimately, how similar we all are in our struggle to understand the eye of the storm and where this hurricane may ultimately take us.

So I hope you enjoy reading their answers and that a few gems might line your way on your music journey.

Bruce Broughton

One of the most versatile composers working today, Bruce Broughton writes in every medium, from theatrical releases and TV feature films to the concert stage and computer games.

His first major film score, for the Lawrence Kasdan western Silverado, *brought him an Oscar nomination. His very next project, a classically styled score for Barry Levinson's* Young Sherlock Holmes, *earned a Grammy nomination for the soundtrack album.*

With more than 20 Emmy nominations, Broughton has received a record 10, most recently for HBO's Warm Springs. *He has also won Emmys for* Eloise at Christmastime; Eloise at The Plaza; Glory & Honor; O Pioneers!; Tiny Toon Adventures Theme Song; The First Olympics, Athens 1896, Part I; Dallas: Ewing Blues; Dallas: The Letter; *and* Buck Rogers: The Satyr. *His score for* Heart of Darkness *was the first orchestral score composed for a video game.*

Broughton is a board member of ASCAP, a governor of the Academy of Motion Picture Arts and Sciences, a former governor of the Academy of Television Arts and Sciences, and past president of the Society of Composers and Lyricists. He has taught film composition in the Advanced Film Music Studies program at USC and is a frequent lecturer at UCLA.

Do you think it is possible to be successful in the "new" music business without relying on a label? (*Success* being defined as "making a living," not necessarily becoming a superstar.)

Obviously, relying on a label in itself was no guarantee of success. At least the "new" business makes it possible for artists to be hands on and centered in their own career paths, while giving one the opportunity to put oneself in the driver's seat.

Is the traditional music business dead?

The traditional method of doing business is certainly wheezing, but it's not dead. All business involves people, networking, distribution, and marketing. Being able to do business digitally is at least an opportunity to market and interface with the client directly. It's like modern warfare: Rather than having to contact your adversary and grapple hand to hand like in the old days, you can now contact thousands without ever seeing who they are, while sitting in a comfortable space with a computer screen, a cup of coffee, and a joystick.

Will CDs eventually disappear completely, displaced by digital files?

CDs will certainly be replaced, and whatever comes afterwards will be replaced as well. Digital files are at greater risk for degradation, modification, and loss than either analog or even paper. In the film industry, a recent report from the Academy of Motion Pictures concluded that modern films are at high risk of loss—perhaps with only a 10-year shelf life—simply because the digital medium is less stable and more likely to soon change. In other words, sprocketed film lasts longer than digital files. Paper books last longer than Kindle. Published music and even vinyl recordings last longer than PDF files or MP3s.

Is placing music on sites such as SoundCloud or ReverbNation a viable way for emerging artists to gain visibility and success in the market?

It's certainly a way to gain visibility, but also to risk having the music taken and distributed for free.

Is "fan funding" a good method for achieving success?

It's one of several ways that might help, but I doubt any method at the moment is bulletproof for success.

Will the music-distribution model change from downloading to streaming? Completely or partially?

Streaming, at least for A/V works, seems the likeliest model for the future. For music itself, downloading seems more likely.

Do you think the current pricing structure for downloading digital music is a good one? (On average, $1.29 for singles, $9.99 for albums.) How about the pricing models for streaming digital music on sites like Spotify or Rdio? (For example, $0.00029 per stream.)

Not too knowledgeable on this one, but obviously at these rates, it takes a lot of sales to get any meaningful income back to the songwriter/composer.

What should be done about protecting intellectual property in the digital age? If SOPA (Stop Online Piracy Act) and PIPA (Protect Intellectual Property Act) are not the answer, what is?

SOPA and PIPA may not be perfect, but they're a start. Music is so popular, it's being stolen. The corporate behemoths like Google and Yahoo! make literally millions of dollars in advertising on pages full of free product. The consumer who ignores the ads simply to get to the product doesn't realize the impact of what it is he/she is taking. The artist whose work has been made available doesn't have the financial means to fight those who distribute it. Often, as in the case of A/V works—film and TV—the artist doesn't even own his product, having already given it away as part of a work-for-hire contract.

Do you believe that music has been devalued in the last 10 years? If so, can anything be done to change the trend?

Music has been devalued to the creator, but certainly not to the distributors. As mentioned above, music is so popular, everyone wants it produced for free. Some creators will simply have to take a big breath and risk saying no. Other than being very careful about contracts and creators' rights before a work is distributed, it's hard to know what direction can be taken that will stop the slide, although self-respect helps.

Do you think that music supervisors are the new A&R people in today's marketplace?

No. Music editors, film editors, producers, directors, and their significant others are the new music supervisors.

What guidance would you give to the emerging artist who is trying to reach some degree of success in today's music market, whether as a musician, songwriter, or composer?

Learn about business and learn how to use the new technology.

Lastly, is there anything else you'd like to add?

Don't dumb your music down, don't give it away, don't be stupid, and don't forget that what you do as a creative person is worth something.

Kari Kimmel

Kari Kimmel's story is one of extremely hard work and intense passion. Originally from South Florida, Kari moved to Los Angeles to pursue her love of music. Since then, she has done everything from writing, recording, and co-producing her own music to placing her songs in more than 200 films and TV shows and has also been named one of the top 50 artists on VH1.com.

Kari's songs and voice have been featured in films and television shows such as Shall We Dance, Footloose, The Hills, White Chicks, Greek, Gilmore Girls, 10 Things I Hate About You, WALL-E, The Young and the Restless, Ella Enchanted, Dreamgirls, The Office, The Bold and the Beautiful, Life Unexpected, America's Funniest Home Videos, Pretty Little Liars, *and* Burn Notice, *to name a few. Her songs have also been used in promos and trailers for the shows* House, 90210, Private Practice, *and* Grey's Anatomy *and the films* Nights in Rodanthe *and* Free Willy 4. *Kari has released four solo albums:* A Life in the Day, Pink Balloon, Out of Focus, *and her latest album,* Go. *She can also be heard on the* Tinkerbell, Princess Disneymania, WALL-E, *and* Ella Enchanted *soundtracks.*

Kari's album Go, *which was released at the end of 2011, is already being heard in numerous films and TV shows. You can hear songs from this album on shows such as* Suburgatory, The Office, Jane by Design, Community, Nine Lives of Chloe King, Make It or Break It, The Real L Word, *and Lifetime's* Carnal Innocence. *Whether you feel like partying or being super introspective, this album has a song for pretty much every emotion you could be feeling or any mood you might be in.*

Do you think it is possible to be successful in the "new" music business without relying on a label? (*Success* being defined as "making a living," not necessarily becoming a superstar.)

I think it's not only possible to be successful in the new music business, but it's way more advantageous than it ever was before. There are so many more outlets for independent musicians now that the Internet is so accessible and viral marketing is available to everybody to a certain degree. It certainly helps to have the money of a record label behind you to fund ad campaigns, go to radio, and properly brand an artist and put them on tour, but it isn't necessary to have a label involved in order to make a living. Remember, the more people that are involved in one's career, the more control that artist must give up.

Is the traditional music business dead?

I don't think it's dead...yet. I think record labels are still extremely powerful because of their structure and the money they have behind them. But because they have so much overhead, there is little room for failure. Back in the day, if a record label believed in an artist and their first single didn't do well—whether it was because of bad timing, lack of proper marketing, or the music itself—they would try again. Now that doesn't happen. If the first single doesn't do *extremely* well, in most cases, that label is done with that artist. So, I think the traditional music business isn't dead, but I think it's very limiting, and it shouldn't be someone's end-all, be-all goal.

Will CDs eventually disappear completely, displaced by digital files?

I don't think people will be releasing their music in CD format for much longer. There is way more cost involved in manufacturing CDs, and the majority of sales are already digital. Maybe CDs will become like records—collectors' items—although I kinda doubt it.

Will the music-distribution model change from downloading to streaming? Completely or partially?

I hope not! If there is any level of inconvenience, people will most likely opt to download rather than stream. As long as the sites that allow you to stream for free—i.e. YouTube, iTunes—come along with some type of annoyance, whether it be commercials, buffering issues, low quality, or needing to stay on a specific site in order to listen to the song, people will most likely continue to download their favorite songs instead of stream for the basic convenience factor.

Do you think the current pricing structure for downloading digital music is a good one? (On average, $1.29 for singles, $9.99 for albums.) How about the pricing models for streaming digital music on sites like Spotify or Rdio? (For example, $0.00029 per stream.)

I think it's working for now. Change in pricing will come when needed—the standard price has already been raised from $0.99 to $1.29.

Do you believe that music has been devalued in the last 10 years? If so, can anything be done to change the trend?

I most definitely think music has been somewhat devalued in that last 10 years, but you can rebel or you can "play ball." Many bands are willing and able to give their music away for free or use the "pay what you want" model. It's not a bad thing per se, but that means artists/bands need to find another way of earning income—not just selling music. Licensing songs to film and TV shows isn't what it used to be, either—fees are way lower and sometimes gratis. Many artists feel that a "gratis" placement devalues their music. It all depends on how you look at it. They can license their song for nothing and possibly get exposure to fans they wouldn't have if they didn't license the song, or they could hold out and hope that a paid license comes along. Personally, I weigh the opportunities and look at the plusses and minuses of licensing that song. If I don't do it, there are thousands of other bands that will. Maybe it's worth it, maybe not. Maybe it devalues the music; maybe it's just playing by the "new rules."

Has getting airplay on Top 40 radio been replaced by licensing music for film or television programs? (Whether it is done directly or through a music library.)

I don't know that it's been replaced, I think it's just another outlet. And for an independent artist, it's a much more attainable outlet.

Do you think that music supervisors are the new A&R people in today's marketplace?

I think music supervisors play a significant role in introducing new bands to the marketplace. For example, the music supervisor for *Grey's Anatomy* played a huge part in helping to break both Snow Patrol and the Fray. Any band lucky enough to get placed on a hit TV show with so many viewers tuning in each week has a great opportunity to catch on with the public. I think having a song in a major national or worldwide commercial also plays a huge role in today's A&R. The Superbowl Kia commercial was mainly responsible for breaking the band the Heavy, and because of the Apple iPad commercial using her song "1, 2, 3, 4," millions of people have now been introduced to Feist. So I would say yes, music supervisors play a huge role as one of the new A&R people in today's marketplace.

What guidance would you give to the emerging artist who is trying to reach some degree of success in today's music market, whether as a musician, songwriter, or composer?

Do as many things *well* as you can. Be proactive, and if at all possible, stay in control of as much as you can. That said, don't be so arrogant that you don't incorporate others into your success. I have had my music placed in over 200 films, TV shows, promos, trailers, and commercials, and while I might do most of it on my own now, I wouldn't be where I am now if I hadn't had the guidance, direction, and help of others along the way.

Nanci M. Walker

Nanci M. Walker is an accomplished record-company executive with more than 20 years of experience with major public and private multinational entertainment companies, such as Columbia Records, EMI Music Publishing, Island/Def Jam Records, and BMG.

She has earned gold records for her work with Pete Yorn, Michael Penn, the Red Jumpsuit Apparatus, and a multi-platinum disc for her work with Cypress Hill. Nanci has established a strong network of contacts throughout the world, including songwriters, recording artists, producers, mixers, record company executives, managers, agents, attorneys, and promoters. She has helped many artists succeed with a focus on ROI and bottom-line objectives.

Nanci has managed the day-to-day publishing business and catalogs of high-profile acts including Beastie Boys, Kenny G, Blink-182, Frank Black/Pixies, and Diana Krall. She has identified, signed, and managed new and existing talent as well as recruited, trained, and supervised A&R scouts nationwide. Nanci has identified brand strategy and identified marketable songs; hired producers, mixers, and engineers; arranged tracking-mixing-mastering sessions for recording projects; and managed multimillion-dollar recording budgets.

Nanci has a Bachelor of Arts degree from Boston College, Chestnut Hill, MA. She has been a frequent speaker or guest teacher at UCLA, the Musician's Institute, Vanderbilt University, and the NMPA (National Music Publisher's Association) in Los Angeles, CA.

Do you think it is possible to be successful in the "new" music business without relying on a label? (*Success* being defined as "making a living," not necessarily becoming a superstar.)

I believe that success is being able to make a living doing what you love—anything beyond that, like becoming a "superstar" or earning a six-figure salary, is icing on the cake. I've been blessed to be able to wake up every morning loving what I do for a living. I wish that for everyone. My advice is that if you have a Plan B, if you can see yourself being in any industry other than the music industry, then you should just go to your Plan B right now. This is a super-competitive business filled with passionate players, be they businesspeople or artists, and only the most persistent, resilient, passionate players survive.

As far as what's being called the "new music business" is concerned, sure, in many ways it's the Wild Wild West out there every time a new technology is introduced, but the basics haven't changed at all: record song, release song, find fans, sell merchandise (whether it be music, T-shirts, concert tickets), make a living. What's new about that?

Is the traditional music business dead?

If you're equating the term "traditional music business" with a model where fans as well as corporations pay artists for music, I think it's too soon to pronounce the "traditional music business" as being dead. The "new music business" is being run by entrepreneurs and phone conglomerates who are often as busy selling advertising space as they are lobbying in Washington D.C. to lower licensing rates for streaming music.

It's the Wild Wild West out there, with a new business sprouting up every day for a land grab. The Internet entrepreneurs proclaim "music for everyone" while they profit from advertising.

Certainly the traditional "delivery system" of music is dead—gone are the warehouses, one-stops, and records stores. We have a great opportunity to deliver music directly to the fans. Now anyone on the planet can be a recording artist and deliver their music in the very same manner as the major record labels. That doesn't mean that they have access to the marketing and promotion teams employed by the "traditional music business."

Will CDs eventually disappear completely, displaced by digital files?

I think that CDs will still serve a purpose as a "value added" item to sell at shows. Vinyl as well…

Is "fan funding" a good method for achieving success?

I guess anyone who sells their music is "fan funded." If a fan chooses to go to iTunes and buy a song, then that artist is "fan funded," right? Or if the fan buys a concert ticket—"fan funded!" I wholly support fan funding. We need to get the word out about it.

Seriously, though, I've seen fan funding work on a pretty small level on the various sites like Kickstarter and PledgeMusic. It's not a good long-term business strategy, but it can help early on in your career. I don't know how many times you can go back to that well before the novelty wears off. Really, those fans contributing money to your cause are patrons. I mean, how many artist careers can one fan support? I know of a musician who sold everything from an autographed CD and a T-shirt to a private show for up to 10 guests to get the funding for a European tour. He got the funding. He had to devote a night to the girl who bought the private show. She arranged for to him come to her apartment in London, and when he got there he was surprised to find that she hadn't invited any guests; it was just her. He pulled out his guitar and played and played and played some more as she watched, and the whole time he was wondering how and when he should end the show. Pretty funny.

Will the music-distribution model change from downloading to streaming? Completely or partially?

I think it's heading toward a subscription model and streaming.

Do you think the current pricing structure for downloading digital music is a good one? (On average, $1.29 for singles, $9.99 for albums.) How about the pricing models for streaming digital music on sites like Spotify or Rdio? (For example, $0.00029 per stream.)

It will be difficult to earn a living on the money you'd currently receive on streaming. The fees will have to be dramatically renegotiated.

What should be done about protecting intellectual property in the digital age? If SOPA (Stop Online Piracy Act) and PIPA (Protect Intellectual Property Act) are not the answer, what is?

The consumer, the fan, has to want to pay for music. I think that the RIAA, NMPA, and the artists themselves need to go into the grade schools and high schools to educate kids about the value of paying for music, movies, and art. The industry should have done that 20 years ago. We missed a great opportunity, and this generation doesn't understand the value of music. We need to appeal to our consumer, not sue them, fine them, and threaten to throw them in jail!

Has getting airplay on Top 40 radio been replaced by licensing music for film or television programs? (Whether it is done directly or through a music library.)

There's a direct link between Top 40 airplay and record sales, and there is a direct link between appearing in a TV show or film and record sales. There's just a lot more record sales connected to Top 40 airplay.

Do you think that music supervisors are the new A&R people in today's marketplace?

Wow, that's an interesting thought. In many ways music supervisors have the ability to tap into new emerging talent long before a label can. In that sense, yes, music supervisors are on the forefront of discovering new music.

Let's please talk about the role of an experienced A&R person. An A&R person does so much more than scout new music. An A&R person helps to choose songs, set up songwriting collaborations, and find the right producer, engineer, mixer, and mastering person. They help set up auditions to put a band together when needed; they advise on image, finding the right video director and photographer. The A&R person is often the person who introduced the artist to his attorney, booking agent, and manager. The A&R person represents the artist within the label, promoting the artist internally to marketing, tour marketing, promotion, and press. All of that input has already taken place long before that music supervisor has heard it—or for that matter, long before that hip DJ who is playing the music is credited with "discovering" it!

What guidance would you give to the emerging artist who is trying to reach some degree of success in today's music market, whether as a musician, songwriter, or composer?

I'd tell them that nothing has changed. There are no shortcuts; you still need to go out there and find your fans, either in person by touring or on the Internet. I would suggest that you start region by region. Think of your career like this: Find a plot of land and plant some seeds. Every week or so, go back to where you planted the seeds and water them. Once your crop has grown and has filled your land, reap your harvest and then expand into the adjoining land, plant more seeds, water, repeat, et cetera.

Even though the world may be at your fingertips via the Internet, I think it's hard to fathom conquering the world. It's daunting; find your niche and grow from there.

Shawn Clement

Shawn K. Clement of Clemistry Music is a film and television composer and one of the most prolific musical artists in Hollywood. From television to film to video games, Shawn has worked in a wide variety of genres and styles, building a vast array of more than 200 credits. He began his professional career helping to originate and develop the musical foundation for the voyeuristic world of reality television—years before the phenomenon saturated the airwaves. Among the original reality television series he has scored are the World's Wildest Police Videos, American Idol, *and* So You Think You Can Dance. *Other notable television series include the cult classic* Buffy the Vampire Slayer, *in which he supplied original songs as well as score. In recognition of his body of work, ASCAP presented him with a Film & Television Music Award for Most Performed Underscore.*

Shawn Clement's past film credits include We Married Margo, Last Chance, *and* Bad Girls from Valley High. *Two recent indie horror films scored by Clement include* Finale *and* Virus X. *He was nominated by the Hollywood Music in Media Awards for* Finale.

His "Wounded Warrior's Hymn" was recently performed at the Kennedy Center as a premiere at the Tribute for Wounded Warriors. The piece received a standing ovation and was performed by a 106-piece orchestra, a 247-member chorus, and Shawn's longtime friend, Jon Anderson (lead singer of Yes). The theme was developed from the score Clement wrote for the animated feature film, Quantum

Quest. *The original score for* Quantum Quest *was recorded at George Lucas' legendary Skywalker Ranch with the San Francisco Philharmonic, also known as the Skywalker Orchestra.*

Clement has new offices at Paramount Pictures, where he is directly involved in a long list of projects for film and television. His company, Clemistry Music, also owns a vast library of more than 2,000 songs and cues. To see his website, please visit www.clemistry.com, and for a complete list of credits, please view his IMDb page at www.imdb.com/name/nm0002996.

Do you think it is possible to be successful in the "new" music business without relying on a label? (*Success* being defined as "making a living," not necessarily becoming a superstar.)

Yes it is, although you need to really think more outside of the box, be more of a businessman than in the past. There are a lot of different potential revenue streams, some more lucrative than others, but you need to do the research and be creative about it.

Is the traditional music business dead?

In most ways it is. I think there's always going to be labels, but the old way of doing business is over. You had all of these over-bloated budgets, all this excess money, these big fat cats—all of this kind of stuff. People making million-dollar records, then the records don't get backed, all of these things we already know about. I think what's happened now with the Internet and all of these technologies we have is that now as an artist you can promote stuff on your own, you can record your own record, release your own record. Really what you need a label for is money to go on tour and money to live on—things like that. But labels are always going to be around because when you see an artist like Lady Gaga, for instance, who is really like a created commodity, that's where the labels are still going to be—breaking these pop icons.

If you're an independent artist or songwriter, you wear all of these hats, but if you get to a certain level, the labels almost become the management, so to speak. Other than that, they don't really serve a function. It's not like they're signing bands today and giving them million-dollar record contracts, because those days are over. And I think they *should* be over, because most of that money was wasted. You shouldn't have to take so much time to make a record. The records you and I grew up with could be made in three days, and those records are still making millions of dollars. So in a way, it's good that the record companies did collapse, because it was a lot of wasted cash. So I think they'll always be around on a certain level, but they're really a distribution arm. So they'll always be there, but they won't be in control. They're not in control now.

Will CDs eventually disappear completely, displaced by digital files?

In my opinion, no. Sort of like records, there will always be a market for them; however, it will be a lot smaller. I prefer to listen to CDs over digital files personally. They sound better to me.

Is placing music on sites such as SoundCloud or ReverbNation a viable way for emerging artists to gain visibility and success in the market?

It's one of the many tools out there to get exposure, but you have to find a way to truly monetize it. There's a good thing and a bad thing about technology. The good thing: Anybody and their grandmother thinks they're an artist now. The bad thing: You have a bunch of crap out there. But if you're smart, and you have something like SoundCloud or whatever, how do you make that part of you making cash as an artist or producer, rather than just sharing it with somebody? I think that's where you have to get creative. Maybe you tease people with a couple of tracks—like the old days, when you released a forty-five or an EP. You get them excited, and then they go buy the main record, using an analogy to old terms. Why not target music supervisors with your SoundCloud demo? In other words, send it out to the right people. I get a lot of people sending me their demos, and I'm thinking why are they sending it to me? I'm a composer, a songwriter—I'm your competition. We've got these tools now, so target who you're going to send your music to.

Is fan funding a good method for achieving success?

Again, it helps. It's one of the newer tools out there. You sort of have to have your fingers in all of the pies.

Will the music-distribution model change from downloading to streaming? Completely or partially?

I believe partially. I mean, I still like records; I still like to listen to CDs. I can't stand when someone sends me an MP3; it sounds like crap, and it's over-compressed. I don't like to download music unless I'm working on a gig and someone says, "Here, listen to this" or something—but for my real listening enjoyment, I want the real thing. Streaming is cool, but what if you want to burn that and play it in your car? And a lot of it depends on where all this technology goes. It takes time for the world to catch up to the same thing and be on the same page, which is why I say "partially." There's always going to be someplace for all these technologies. Then there are always these diehards, like me. People say they're going to send me an MP3, and I say no, send me a CD—and they think I'm out of my mind. Or they say, "Go to my site and listen to it," and I say, "No, I don't want to hear it in that light." Will it ever get to where it all sounds pristine? Maybe further down the pike. I mean, we have the technology, but people want it quick, fast, now, and cheap.

Do you think the current pricing structure for downloading digital music is a good one? (On average, $1.29 for singles, $9.99 for albums.) How about the pricing models for streaming digital music on sites like Spotify or Rdio? (For example, $0.00029 per stream.)

I think that is fine; however, the real issue with the streaming is performance-royalty income.

What should be done about protecting intellectual property in the digital age? If SOPA (Stop Online Piracy Act) and PIPA (Protect Intellectual Property Act) are not the answer, what is?

Tough to answer. I do feel, though, that technologies such as watermarking and fingerprinting are part of the answer. Tracking all of the uses is more important than ever, and again, we need laws in place that truly protect copyright holders and music creators.

Do you believe that music has been devalued in the last 10 years? If so, can anything be done to change the trend?

It definitely has. The problem is that there is a perception that music is "free." There needs to be a change in attitude from the general public, and we need laws and such to protect music creators' rights.

People are driving along in their car listening to music, and they're thinking, "These people making this music are already rich. Why do they need more money?" They don't understand that some musicians only make these royalties, and without them, well, we're not all rich, and many are struggling.

A lot of these attitudes are unique to America, because when you go over to Europe, for example, artists are regarded as incredible people because what we do touches everybody. It's not like we make Coca-Cola and some people like Coca-Cola. In America, they assume all artists are rich, but we're not—and we're providing a service that's unique, that's special, and that's how we make our money. Laws need to change, copyrights need to be upheld, but they need to be enforced. How do you do that? I don't know—call your senator or your congressman. But when it comes to devaluing your music, composers are the worst—they'll work for free. How is anybody supposed to think you're worth anything if you work for free? I think the artists themselves need to stick up for themselves. And I love it when artists pull their music from Spotify and others because they're saying, "No, I value my music. I have a good product, and I've worked hard for this." It's a complicated issue, but the bottom line is that most of us are not rich—hey, lots of musicians are just trying to make rent!

Has getting airplay on Top 40 radio been replaced by licensing music for film or television programs? (Whether it is done directly or through a music library.)

I don't think so 100 percent, but I believe that artists are realizing that that is where the real money is, especially since the collapse of the record industry.

Do you think that music supervisors are the new A&R people in today's marketplace?

In a way, yes. I also think that the huge growth in video games is where artists are able to get real exposure and help drive the other components of their portfolio, if you will.

What guidance would you give to the emerging artist who is trying to reach some degree of success in today's music market, whether as a musician, songwriter, or composer?

I would say for starters, understand that this is a business! You have to really understand the game that you're in. Utilize all the resources that are out there, and these days we have tons of tools. Think outside the box and also remember that it is still a relationship business as well. Also, especially with composers, you're part of a system or project. It's a lot of teamwork. Be prepared to listen and learn at all times. There is a ton of collaboration here. It takes hard work, 150 percent minimum, 24/7. There is more competition out there than there has ever been, and it keeps getting greater. The business is not for everyone, so make sure that you're prepared to make the sacrifices and spend the time to get where you want to go.

Lastly, is there anything else you'd like to add?

Well, in today's industry you really have to be educated in all the aforementioned aspects. Take the time to understand this stuff. With all the resources out there, there really is no excuse for people to sign bad deals or not realize how things get paid. Do the work.

Marco Alpert

Initially a film composer and theatrical sound designer, Marco Alpert has spent more than 30 years conceptualizing and marketing musical instrument and recording technology products. Starting at E-MU Systems in the late 1970s, he helped drive the adoption of digital sampling as a key technology of music production. In the mid-1990s, he joined Akai Professional as a strategic marketing consultant, where he conceived and oversaw the introduction of the iconic MPC2000 beat production workstation. Since 1998, he has been the marketing guy at Antares Audio Technologies, helping to make Auto-Tune remain a pop-culture phenomenon and, incidentally, forever changing the practice of vocal production. Most recently, Marco and the rest of the Antares team are hard at work doing the same for guitar. Marco still buys CDs.

Is the traditional music business dead?

If by "traditional" one means the business where people get their music on CDs that they buy at their local record store (do those even exist anymore?) or from Amazon or wherever, then no, it's not quite dead, but it's definitely on life support. And the prognosis is pretty grim.

Will CDs eventually disappear completely, displaced by digital files?

Probably not completely, at least not too soon, but they'll become a smaller and smaller niche, as vinyl is now. While most people seem quite content to trade absolute audio quality for convenience, there will always be some unwilling to make that compromise. It seems to me to be inevitable that digital downloads and streaming will eventually be capable of "audiophile" quality for those who desire it, but until then, some will want better than what they offer today. And, of course, there are still people who want to buy their music on something they can hold in their hands and stack on their shelves. (And can you imagine those folks with their loony music systems with $500 power cables and $3,000 speaker cables wanting to demo them with iTunes Store downloads?)

Will the music-distribution model change from downloading to streaming?

It won't for me. Can't speak for the kids (who darn well better keep off my lawn).

Do you believe that music has been devalued in the last 10 years?

Depends what one means by "devalued." If meant in a business sense—i.e., something with value that people are willing to pay for—then definitely. Just hang around high school kids. The very idea of paying for music is preposterous to most of them. Most have iPods and iPhones filled with thousands of songs, few paid for. Where to find them to download free is common knowledge. I have no idea who's buying all those songs from the iTunes Store.

If, however, one means that music has been devalued as an important commodity in people's lives, then no. It's as important as ever. If anything, now that one can have virtually their entire music library with them at all times, it's even a bigger part of their lives.

Shawn LeMone

Shawn LeMone is vice president and general manager of the Film & Television / Visual Media department in ASCAP's Membership Group. Shawn advocates on behalf of film, television, and video game composers and resolves high-level crediting and distribution issues. His department is responsible for servicing ASCAP's composer members and maintaining a strong market share across all audio-visual mediums.

Having joined the society's Los Angeles office in 1995, LeMone has spearheaded ASCAP's outreach efforts to the film and television production community and the video game industry. He has been instrumental in the development of industry standards for television performance data and educating production companies on the role of performance rights. In addition, he is among those at the forefront of ASCAP's efforts to explore and employ strategic and technological innovations to better serve its composer and publisher members.

Prior to ASCAP, LeMone served as the Foreign Levies Administrator for both the Directors Guild of America (DGA) and the Writers Guild of America (WGA) from 1991 to 1995. During his tenure at the guilds, he developed and administered a large royalty account derived from levies on the sale and rental of video tape in Europe.

LeMone graduated from UCLA in 1991 with a degree in social psychology and is a dormant guitarist and songwriter. He has organized and participated in seminars at UCLA, the Society of Composers and Lyricists, American Film Institute, Game Developers Conference, Austin Music Foundation, California Lawyers for the Arts, and the California Copyright Conference, where he served as president of the Board of Directors.

Do you think it is possible to be successful in the "new" music business without relying on a label? (Success being defined as "making a living," not necessarily becoming a superstar.)

I think is it more possible to be successful as an independent musician without label support than ever before. One has to be industrious and exercise a lot of initiative, though, to make it in the new marketplace. You have to be a master of all media and try to get your music placed in as many different outlets as possible.

Is the traditional music business dead?

As we once knew it, yes. Publishers and especially labels have had to reinvent themselves. There is much more emphasis on licensing and touring over sales. New players have entered the marketplace and will continue to do so as it evolves further. The role of performing rights organizations in keeping the music industry monetized is more important than ever before.

Will CDs eventually disappear completely, displaced by digital files?

Probably. CDs are just digital media distributed on a big shiny disc instead of between devices, and I don't think there is the same consumer attachment to CDs that there is to vinyl, which is making a curious comeback in some circles.

Will the music-distribution model change from downloading to streaming? Completely or partially?

The mode of distribution for all entertainment products is moving from downloading to streaming. We are gradually evolving from a culture of ownership to a culture of access. Once access to entertainment products is ubiquitous, there will be less of a compelling need to pay the extra premium required to own your own personal copies of media files.

What should be done about protecting intellectual property in the digital age? If SOPA (Stop Online Piracy Act) and PIPA (Protect Intellectual Property Act) are not the answer, what is?

I believe many of the central concepts of these bills will emerge in new bills that will eventually pass. Our most important export as a nation is intellectual property. Once the hysteria has subsided, rational minds will prevail, and stronger copyright protection will be implemented.

Do you believe that music has been devalued in the last 10 years? If so, can anything be done to change the trend?

Yes. The irony is that music is a more ever-present part of people's lives than ever before. I think there is a chance that American pop culture may correct itself on the value of music as more artists use the new technology to create meaningful relationships with their listeners and more awareness of the work that goes into being a professional musician is put out there.

Has getting airplay on Top 40 radio been replaced by licensing music for film or television programs? (Whether it is done directly or through a music library.)

It has not replaced it, but more bands and artists are looking to gain exposure for their music through placement in film and television than ever before. There has been an explosion of opportunities for music placement in audio-visual. It can still be an important distinction to have a song place on Top 40 radio.

Do you think that music supervisors are the new A&R people in today's marketplace?

Not quite. Music supervisors don't do all the support work that A&R execs at labels traditionally have done. Music supervisors are certainly important tastemakers, though, and because of the value being placed on licensing songs for film and television, their visibility within the industry has risen. There is still a separate need for artist development. A lot of ASCAP members have been looking increasingly to us for this kind of support.

What guidance would you give to the emerging artist who is trying to reach some degree of success in today's music market, whether as a musician, songwriter, or composer?

Be true to yourself. Write music that comes from your soul. Don't try to emulate the latest trend. Once you have produced some great music, use every asset at your disposal to get it out there and be heard. Make lots of friends. No one will ever hear your music if you're locked away in your studio all the time, no matter how great it is.

Jim Aikin

Jim Aikin spent 25 years on the editorial staff of Keyboard *magazine. Since being downsized in 2002, he has written innumerable freelance articles for* Keyboard, Electronic Musician, Mix, *and other music magazines, as well as four books (*Power Tools for Synthesizer Programming *[Backbeat/Hal Leonard],* Chords & Harmony *[Backbeat/Hal Leonard],* Picture Yourself Playing Cello *[Course Technology PTR], and* Csound Power! *[Course Technology PTR]). Currently, he teaches cello privately in Northern California and is the principal cellist in two community orchestras—but he still loves synthesizers!*

Do you think it is possible to be successful in the "new" music business without relying on a label? (*Success* being defined as "making a living," not necessarily becoming a superstar.)

If by "label" you mean a corporate-owned major label, I would hazard a guess that your chances of success are at least as good doing it on your own as trying to make it in the "big leagues," and possibly a whole lot better. First, you'll have far more artistic control, which means you'll almost certainly be happier, even if you never rake in the big bucks. Second, you will be able to make your own career decisions about where to play, who to collaborate with, and so on. Third, you'll retain a much larger percentage of the royalties!

That's not to say it will be a piece of cake. You'll need to wear a lot of hats—not only musician, composer, and recording engineer, but also publisher, distributor, promoter, web designer, and booking agent. But here's the good news: If you wear all of those hats for a couple of years and build up a real following, when the major labels come knocking at your door (a) you won't be starstruck into thinking you can't live without them, and (b) you'll be able to evaluate whatever deal they offer you much more realistically, because you'll understand the business.

Is the traditional music business dead?

As long as there are Van Halen tribute bands filling stadiums, I would have to say no. It's not dead. But I'm pretty sure it's pinin' for the fjords. (That's an old Monty Python line—am I showing my age?) Being corporate-owned, the major labels have shown a consistent inability to adopt new business models. But I'm purely a spectator in this process. I have no inside information.

Will CDs eventually disappear completely, displaced by digital files?

No. If you look at the profit margin from selling a physical CD, an indie band can do much, much better economically by selling CDs than by selling downloads through iTunes or any other online digital distributor. There's also the "hit single" problem to consider. If you have one great song and nine more songs that are good but not quite as riveting, when you put them all on a CD, the great song will sell the whole $20 CD. In Downloadville, you'll be selling that one 99-cent song, and the other songs won't sell. For both reasons, physical CDs will continue to be viable as a way for artists to distribute their work.

Is placing music on sites such as SoundCloud or ReverbNation a viable way for emerging artists to gain visibility and success in the market?

I don't know, but I'm pretty sure it depends on the artist. I'm a big fan of Pomplamoose, and they gained tremendous visibility on YouTube—but they did it by being really, really smart, not just by uploading home-brew videos. (a) They did covers of well-known tunes, so that fans of Lady Gaga or whoever would find Pomplamoose. (b) Their roots-rock arrangements are consistently solid, and their original songs are brilliant. (c) Nataly Dawn is cute. (d) Their "no lip-sync" video ethic was unique and made the music seem more honest. (e) Nataly is also a very good video editor.

Would YouTube work as well for breaking your band? Gee, I don't know. What have you got to put on the table that would compare with that set of positive factors?

Is fan funding a good method for achieving success?

You mean through Kickstarter? I have no idea. Has anyone succeeded using this method? If so, you should ask them how they did it.

Will the music-distribution model change from downloading to streaming? Completely or partially?

Predicting the future is a fun parlor game, but here's a flash: Nobody has a freakin' clue what will happen in the future. Questions of this sort have no real value, in my opinion. I have to say, though, I love Pandora. My Pandora "channel" is defined by Weather Report, so whenever I'm at the gym my phone is streaming '80s jazz fusion nonstop. This is wonderful, because I don't have to pick tunes or manage the storage of my music library. Whether it's wonderful for the surviving musicians of that era is an entirely different question. I have no idea what Pandora's revenue model is, but based on how few ads I hear in the free streaming app, I'd hazard a guess that George Duke and Jean-Luc Ponty are probably not rolling in royalties from Pandora.

Do you think the current pricing structure for downloading digital music is a good one? (On average, $1.29 for singles, $9.99 for albums.) How about the pricing models for streaming digital music on sites like Spotify or Rdio? (For example, $0.00029 per stream.)

I'm not qualified to comment in this area, but I did see a graphic online today that strongly suggests that Spotify sucks in terms of its ability to provide musicians anything resembling a living wage.

What should be done about protecting intellectual property in the digital age? If SOPA (Stop Online Piracy Act) and PIPA (Protect Intellectual Property Act) are not the answer, what is?

I'm not sure there *is* an answer, but I'm pretty sure that turning your fans into criminals isn't it. In order to give you a one-sentence answer, I have to begin with two sentences of preamble. First, I'm a strong supporter of unions and union workers. Second, the Musicians' Union is a completely useless wheeze. That said, the Union's venerable slogan is entirely apropos: "Always insist on live music." What musicians can do that cannot be digitally cloned is *perform*.

In the 1980s, the Grateful Dead made no attempt whatsoever to control the copies that were being made of their music. There was a whole fan underground that bought and sold bootleg Dead records.

They had a whole darn *section* set up at their concerts for people to set up recording gear to make bootlegs. And you know what? That band was phenomenally successful as a business enterprise.

The lesson I would pick up from this is that if your fans are swapping digital files of your songs by the boatload, then when your tour comes through town, you'll be selling concert tickets by the boatload. And you'll probably be selling CDs by the boatload, too. A CD offers the fan a tangible object. It's collectible. A digital download is not collectible. It's dust in the wind.

Do you believe that music has been devalued in the last 10 years? If so, can anything be done to change the trend?

I think we need to take the broad view here, and not get too hypnotized by consumer mood swings. Next week I'll be playing a concert with a community orchestra (actually, two concerts back to back, one on Saturday night, the next on Sunday afternoon), at which we will be performing Beethoven's Seventh Symphony for several hundred people. I very much doubt that any of those people will feel that either Beethoven or music in general has been devalued in the last 10 years.

From what I've read and heard, the club scene is in pretty dismal shape. Far too many club owners expect musicians to play for free. And then there are the deejays.... If the Union weren't such a joke, it could do something about this.

Has getting airplay on Top 40 radio been replaced by licensing music for film or television programs? (Whether it is done directly or through a music library.)

I'm not really qualified to speak about the relative merits of Top 40 versus licensing as ways to establish a career and bring in money, but my best guess is that there are more market opportunities in licensing, simply because Top 40 is such a tight business. But then, I've never tried to hustle a track for TV. Maybe it's just as bad. There are a lot more cable channels than Top 40 channels, though, that's pretty clear—and they all need music, don't they?

What guidance would you give to the emerging artist who is trying to reach some degree of success in today's music market, whether as a musician, songwriter, or composer?

First, evaluate your strengths and weaknesses realistically. In other words, don't buy your own bull! If you're weak in certain areas, figure out how you can get better—or figure out how to play to your strengths and downplay your weaknesses. There are a heck of a lot of wannabe musicians in the world who have neither a prayer nor a clue. Don't be one of them.

Second, understand the realities of the world in which you'll be hustling to make a buck. Don't be naive about money, contracts, or the competition. If you're making baskets of money this year, invest it wisely! Chances are, you won't be making the same kind of money when you're 50 or 60.

Third, always operate in a professional manner. Don't make excuses or cut corners. Be courteous to those with whom you have business relationships.

Fourth—and you're going to hate this—don't give up your day job. Realistically, there are 10 times as many talented pop musicians in the world as there are career opportunities. Being optimistic about your chances is essential, but while you're being optimistic, keep the door open for unexpected opportunities. While working toward success as an artist, you may find yourself teaching music lessons, working in a retail music store, running the sound system for worship services, doing sound design for a synthesizer manufacturer, or (as in my case) working at a music magazine. And strange as it may seem, once the sense of futility has worn off, you may find that that's the right place for you. You may be able to make a very significant musical contribution to the world year after year, even if nobody ever hears your original songs.

One of my favorite artists is Robert Rich. He has released more than a dozen CDs on his own label, and he tours as a solo act. But if you go to his website, click on the Studio tab, and scroll to the bottom of the page, you'll find a long, long list of mixing and mastering credits. I don't know exactly what Robert's revenue stream looks like, but it's clear he brings in significant money by recording and mixing *other* people's music. That's part of his career. And I'm sure this opens up opportunities for various kinds of artistic synergy, as well as keeping his mixing and mastering chops sharp for when it's time to do his own CDs.

There's a lesson here.

Lastly, is there anything else you'd like to add?

A couple of things, since you asked.

First, drinking and using while playing a gig is (a) not even faintly professional and (b) a case of buying your own bull. If you think you play better when you've had a glass of wine to loosen up, my advice is, stop drinking and take some darn lessons.

Second, I don't care what anybody says—a deejay is not a musician. A musician is a person who, if you're on the bandstand and the guy next to you says, "Okay, blues in A! One—two—one-two-three-four…," you can jump straight in and play it, and sound okay, and not make them want to throw you off the stage. A bongo player is a musician. An accordion player is a musician. Even banjo players are musicians. Bagpipes I'm not too sure about, because they can only play in one key, but we'll give them a pass on that. Or, if you're a classical player, somebody puts a page full of dots down in front of you and waves a stick, and you can play the dots with reasonable precision. Or, if it's just you and the computer, you can sit down and make up new, original music out of thin air…without using sampled loops. If you can do any of that, you're a musician.

How many deejays do you know who can sit down and blow a blues in A? How many deejays do you know who can play the dots while the guy up at the front of the orchestra waves a stick? Not many, I'll bet.

And that's entirely enough out of me.

Randy Wachtler

Randy Wachtler is the president/founder and composer of 615 Music Companies, headquartered in Nashville, Tennessee, with affiliated offices in Los Angeles. Additionally, he is EVP of Warner/Chappell Production Music.

In addition to his role as head of 615 Music, Randy is currently the chairman and a member of the Board of Directors of the Production Music Association (PMA), based in Los Angeles.

Born and raised in Minneapolis, Minnesota, where he started playing drums in local bands, Randy then moved to Tampa, Florida, where he continued to tour with regional bands. He studied at the University of South Florida and played drums in several touring groups throughout the Southeast for four years. In 1980, Randy moved to Nashville, where he continued his studies in recording industry management at Middle Tennessee State University (MTSU).

Upon graduation from MTSU in 1984, Randy founded 615 Music Productions. Since its founding, 615 Music has become a full-service commercial music-production company and world leader in the creation of music for advertisers, television networks, TV and radio stations, interactive media, and cable worldwide.

615 Music's production music division specializes in composing and distributing several production music catalogues, including the Platinum collection, Promo Accelerator, Metro, Gold Series, Scoring Stage, Ultimate Crime and Drama, Minimal Music, Kingsize, and Song Street Records, with other distributed libraries including AMP, ZEN, Music Shop, and Music Gallery. Collectively, the company's catalogues feature more than 40,000 tracks across 23 production catalogues available for license to film and TV productions, theatrical trailers, and corporate and A/V productions. The library is currently distributed in more than 68 countries globally.

Do you think it is possible to be successful in the "new" music business without relying on a label? (Success being defined as "making a living," not necessarily becoming a superstar.)

I believe labels provide a valuable service to artists, and from what I've seen, labels have been evolving recently to be even more attractive to artists.

I don't really work on the artists and label side, so my observations are probably not as relevant as those of someone working directly within those realms.

Is the traditional music business dead?

I don't believe the traditional music business is dead. It's redefining itself as we speak.

Are placements with music libraries supplanting traditional avenues for composers and songwriters to break into the business?

Yes, we have many talented new and established composers and songwriters who contribute to the library business as an addition to their current work, but also some of them make quite a good living composing for library only.

Will CDs eventually disappear completely, displaced by digital files?

It's likely that some people will always like to collect physical product, but there's no doubt digital is the future.

Is placing music on sites such as SoundCloud or ReverbNation a viable way for emerging artists to gain visibility and success in the market?

I believe those are good tools to use, but I caution composers and songwriters to not blindly put their music on the Internet. There is so much theft that one needs to be careful about how they distribute their copyrights.

Will the music distribution model change from downloading to streaming? Completely or partially?

The new "cloud" concept of streaming or leasing music is an interesting one. As long as creators are compensated fairly for the use of their creations, whether it's through downloading or streaming, then I'm all for it.

What should be done about protecting intellectual property in the digital age? If SOPA (Stop Online Piracy Act) and PIPA (Protect Intellectual Property Act) are not the answer, what is?

Copyright laws need to evolve in the digital age where creators are fairly compensated for their work; otherwise, a lot of creative people won't be able to make a living, and our culture will suffer. We must protect composers and songwriters and their works so we can continue to enjoy their valuable contributions to our society.

Do you believe that music has been devalued in the last 10 years? If so, can anything be done to change the trend?

Yes, music has been devalued by illegal downloading and sharing. If you obtain someone else's creation without paying for it, that is stealing and it's against the law in this country. We have laws against this type of practice, and the legal system will deal with people who break the law.

Has getting airplay on Top 40 radio been replaced by licensing music for film or television programs? (Whether it is done directly or through a music library.)

I don't think it's been replaced. Radio airplay is still an important part of an artist's career.

Do you think that music supervisors are the new A&R people in today's marketplace?

Some of them are for sure, and the good ones spot great new talent.

What guidance would you give to the emerging artist who is trying to reach some degree of success in today's music market, whether as a musician, songwriter, or composer?

It's sounds so cliché, but it's important to be true to yourself as an artist. Those that do seem to emerge as unique, interesting artists, and the marketplace seems to respond to those kinds of artists. Know your rights and associate with reputable production music libraries that have a track record and that belong to the PMA (Production Music Association). The PMA has consistently shown they have the more reputable libraries as members.

Lastly, is there anything else you'd like to add?

People love music and always will. Always remember that.

Philip G. Antoniades

A DIY pioneer and honors graduate of the Berklee College of Music, Philip Antoniades focuses on finding innovative business solutions that create income for musicians. With 20+ years of experience, he knows many facets of the music industry, having toured nationally as a drummer, owned a record label, managed artists, produced records, and promoted shows.

In the '90s, Philip started Johnny Brock Management, a New England agency, managing a group of singer-songwriters including Barbara Kessler and Peter Mulvey, as well as founding the International Boston Acoustic Underground Competition. In 1996, he founded Artist Development Associates, providing mastering, CD manufacturing, design, and promotion services to independent touring artists. In 1997, Philip launched CDFreedom.com to provide an online retail venue for fulfillment of CDs and other merchandise to a growing indie customer base. In 2004, he merged Artist Development Associates with Nimbit in the pursuit of delivering artists a direct relationship with their fans. He has continued to pursue his passion as president and chief product officer for Nimbit's products.

Philip's passion for creating innovative direct-to-fan connections can be traced as far back as 1996, when Billboard *covered Barbara Kessler's successful CD-of-the-month-club fan subscription program. Known for his hands-on, direct, and practical approach, Phil is frequently a speaker and moderator on industry panels, including SXSW, Berklee College of Music, Belfast Music Week, Harvard Business School, New Music Seminar NY & LA, Cutting Edge Music, Boston Higher Education, Leadership Music Summit, Nashville, TECHnically Music, CMJ, NEMO, NERFA, Boston Music Conference, NARM, ASCAP Expo LA & NY, the Miami Digital Music Conference, SF Bandwidth, and more. He has a BA in Percussion/Music Synthesis, Magna Cum Laude, Berklee College of Music.*

Do you think it is possible to be successful in the "new" music business without relying on a label? (*Success* being defined as "making a living," not necessarily becoming a superstar.)

The simple answer is yes. The longer answer is that some entrepreneurial artists will have no trouble building a career. Other artists may need help from a team or manager, but the concept of relying on a label in the traditional model doesn't make any sense anymore.

Is the traditional music business dead?

Yes. It can no longer harness and control the income streams that once fed it. It's done.

Are placements with music libraries supplanting traditional avenues for composers and songwriters to break into the business?

The expanding use of music with media is certainly creating more opportunities for exposure and added income. How well the artist is prepared to take advantage of the exposure is a determining factor in leveraging any break. As with any part of the music business that shows any chance to make money or gain exposure, it's getting noisy, artists are getting exploited, and licenses are going down in value.

Will CDs eventually disappear completely, displaced by digital files?

I ran a successful business as a CD manufacturing broker for all of the '90s. If you asked me this question 10 years ago, I'd have said, "CDs will be gone in a couple of years." At this point I'm not so sure. They are a very inexpensive way to get digital content into the hands of your fans at shows. They are still a collectable. My band sells a lot of CDs at shows. The "pay what you want" model gets us an average of $7.50 a CD, and we sell tons of them! (It ain't over 'til it's over.) Fans are pretty confused right now about how to consume music. There are tons of ways to do it: steal it, download, subscribe, buy direct, etc. But fans want to support artists, and buying a CD is an easy way for them to show their support.

Is placing music on sites such as SoundCloud or ReverbNation a viable way for emerging artists to gain visibility and success in the market?

They are great services, but I don't think they are the answer. I have faith in the fact that some 10-year-old kid is going to define a new paradigm for discovering music. But, I think the Spotify/Facebook integration is the first real innovation in changing the way we discover music. It's too bad that Spotify doesn't look like it will produce enough of an income stream for the content creators.

Is fan funding a good method for achieving success?

It's not a method of achieving success. Crowd sourcing is a great concept. Fans want to support artists. They want to be a part of the process. They want to be taken along for the ride. What's critical about crowd sourcing is how you treat your crowd. What I'm afraid of is that most artists don't really understand their responsibility to involve their fans and to deliver. And the outcome may sour fan funding after fans are let down one too many times.

Will the music-distribution model change from downloading to streaming? Completely or partially?

I think it's too early to tell. Streaming doesn't look like it will create enough income to support the business of making music. But technologically, it makes sense that music be consumed from one giant library. I don't think the world has the bandwidth to handle all music consumption as a stream.

Do you think the current pricing structure for downloading digital music is a good one? (On average, $1.29 for singles, $9.99 for albums.) How about the pricing models for streaming digital music on sites like Spotify or Rdio? (For example, $0.00029 per stream.)

The price of music or any commodity is determined by what the market will pay. I think this is comparing apples to oranges. Fans pay $1.29 to iTunes, but the artist receives no more than 70 percent of that money and in most cases less. With the streaming model, the payout to the artist is $.0029 per play. That isn't a purchase but more of a broadcast royalty, and it's not a replacement for the income that would have been generated from downloads.

What should be done about protecting intellectual property in the digital age? If SOPA (Stop Online Piracy Act) and PIPA (Protect Intellectual Property Act) are not the answer, what is?

In my dream scenario, everyone would simply pay an IP tax on their cable bill. Charge a penny for every file downloaded that is registered and considered licensed IP. I pay $180 a month for my cable, phone, and Internet. I wouldn't care about an extra $1 fee for the 1,000 files I downloaded or watched or listened to. But that could create real income. I believe all the technology to track and pay the tax exists! It would encourage file sharing. It would encourage consumption.

Do you believe that music has been devalued in the last 10 years? If so, can anything be done to change the trend?

Yes. Music is still one of the few products that consumers create an emotional connection to.

Has getting airplay on Top 40 radio been replaced by licensing music for film or television programs? (Whether it is done directly or through a music library.)

Licensing has created new channels for exposure to lots of unsigned artists that would never make it to Top 40. It hasn't replaced radio. Radio is still effective but doesn't drive the sales it used to.

Do you think that music supervisors are the new A&R people in today's marketplace?

They certainly play an interesting role in determining what artists will get exposure, but they would only be replacing A&R roles if they were actually participating in the artist's business as a partner.

What guidance would you give to the emerging artist who is trying to reach some degree of success in today's music market, whether as a musician, songwriter, or composer?

The new model for the music business is years away. It's not at all clear what that business will look like or how music will be consumed. But music has value, and some genius will figure out how to harness that value again. Technology has done wonderful things to make it easier than ever to create music as well as get you worldwide exposure in minutes! It has never been more important to find your originality, master your craft, and hone your performance skills. What makes you different is what will set you apart in this world. In addition, your fans are your future. Know them. Communicate with them through your music and directly in person and through social networking.

Lastly, is there anything else you'd like to add?

When the old business finally implodes, a new one will emerge. I believe we haven't seen even a taste of what the new business will look like, but I know that fans have always patronized artists, long before the record business existed. The emotional connection of a fan to their favorite music can never be denied, and it's never been easier to create ways for fans to support you. There will be a future; we just aren't there yet!

Ariel Hyatt

Ariel Hyatt is a thought leader in the digital PR world: the founder of a successful PR firm, international speaker and educator, and the author of two books on social media and marketing for artists. Ariel's Cyber PR® process marks the intersection of social media with engaged behavior, PR, and online marketing. She developed her platform, Cyber PR, to automate much of the traditional PR process and maximize client placement with new media makers.

Ariel's biweekly newsletter and YouTube series, SoundAdvice, has attracted more than 20,000 subscribers, and she has penned more than 100 articles to date. Ariel is also the author of two successful books on PR and new media: Music Success in Nine Weeks (Ariel Publicity, 2008) and Musician's Roadmap to Facebook & Twitter (Ariel Publicity, 2011), which offer artists a step-by-step plan to create a profitable and sustainable business from their art.

Ariel has been invited to speak at festivals and conferences including SXSW, CMJ, ASCAP's I Create Music, the Future of Music, Canadian Music Week, APRA's Song Summit (Sydney), You Are in Control (Reykjavik), the ECMAs, NARAS, Grammy Camp, and the Taxi Road Rally.

Ariel proudly serves on the advisory boards of Sweet Relief Musicians Fund, SXSW Accelerator, SoundCtrl, and the New Music Seminar. She is an obsessive world traveler, a total foodie, and a vintage lunchbox collector.

Do you think it is possible to be successful in the "new" music business without relying on a label? (*Success* being defined as "making a living," not necessarily becoming a superstar.)

It's a myth that you need a label to achieve success. For the past 18 years, the many artists I have worked with have made healthy livings without a label. What you need is, first and foremost, *great music*. Then after that, you need a plan, an infrastructure that works, and perseverance. It is my hope that artists grasp that becoming a "superstar" is a one-in-a-million occurrence (not that this should not be a goal if that's what you want). I think the best that all of us can hope for in this industry is making a living from making our art, and I believe that will happen to more and more artists as things settle, systems get mastered, and more opportunities arise.

Is the traditional music business dead?

There are aspects of the traditional music business that are absolutely not dead. Certain things still apply and still work. For example you will never get on national mainstream radio in heavy rotation without label support. I think the "plug and play" music business that we used to know so well, where you could follow a formula and win, is indeed dead. I do see new standards beginning to arise, and this is encouraging.

Will CDs eventually disappear completely, displaced by digital files?

I'm afraid that's how it's looking these days. I don't know if digital files will be the absolute answer. I think we need to take the cloud and services like Spotify and Rdio into consideration as well.

Is placing music on sites such as SoundCloud or ReverbNation a viable way for emerging artists to gain visibility and success in the market?

Absolutely! I've seen multiple artists placing music on SoundCloud and ReverbNation and sharing tracks with tastemakers and fans. This can enable a viral spread through a tight-knit group of engaged fans and pick-up onto blogs.

In our current environment, fans are expecting music for free. So by uploading your music to these sites, artists are creating fabulous goodwill and effective self-promotion. It's a win-win.

Is fan funding a good method for achieving success?

I am a strong believer in fan funding, as it's a fabulous way to get a project that you're longing to do off the ground, that you may not have money to fund (such as creating an album, making a video, or getting tour support). I'm seeing fan funding step in where traditional record labels used assist artists.

I believe there is no harm in asking your fans to support your dreams and to help you get there. Some artists I work with say that they feel like carnival barkers when asking their fans for money. Others have gotten more comfortable with it. The problem that I foresee with fan funding for the long term is that artists need to be careful about how many times they keep going back to a core group of fans to ask them for money.

Will the music-distribution model change from downloading to streaming? Completely or partially?

I am not really a streaming expert, but certainly, you can see with the meteoric rise of sites like Spotify and Rdio that people love streaming. It's easy, it puts everything at your fingertips, and as smartphones and computers and devices get easier and easier to integrate, it's very, very hard to ask people to download and pay money when they can have unlimited streaming for free.

However, I think there will always be people who want to own music and want to have it downloaded. Also, streaming doesn't work in the subway. Streaming doesn't work when you're out of cell range. So, I think downloading is definitely here to stay at least for some time.

Do you think the current pricing structure for downloading digital music is a good one? (On average, $1.29 for singles, $9.99 for albums.) How about the pricing models for streaming digital music on sites like Spotify or Rdio? (For example, $0.00029 per stream.)

$9.99 for an album is a lot of money to part with when you can pay $8 a month or $9 a month for Spotify and get unlimited music and then purchase the few tracks that actually resonate with you. Also, artists are giving away previews and downloads in droves, so I think the current pricing structure can't sustain over the long haul.

Do you believe that music has been devalued in the last 10 years? If so, can anything be done to change the trend?

Yes, of course it has. I believe that anyone who punishes fans for doing things that they don't see as illegal is asking for trouble down the line. The new paradigm is here to stay, and I'm not sure anything can be done to change the trend. Creative marketing and creating value in other ways is necessary, and I believe the only way out.

Has getting airplay on Top 40 radio been replaced by licensing music for film or television programs? (Whether it is done directly or through a music library.)

Not in the eyes of an artist. I still have met very few who don't want the dream of hearing themselves playing on every station coast to coat for mass exposure. Of course, smart artists also want film and TV licensing for the big paychecks that can be associated with it, but a dream is a dream.

Do you think that music supervisors are the new A&R people in today's marketplace?

As far as people who have the power to affect a musician's bottom line (get money into their pockets), I believe that music supervisors are more powerful than A&R people ever were if you consider the percentage of artists who actually succeeded who were signed by A&R versus the amount of money going into artists' pockets with film and TV deals.

What guidance would you give to the emerging artist who is trying to reach some degree of success in today's music market, whether as a musician, songwriter, or composer?

No one is going to come and save you in today's wild west. It's entirely up to the artist now to make it happen.

I want to end with a quote that inspires my staff and me every day, and I believe it's the artists who are willing to learn who will create sustainable careers for themselves over the long term.

"In a time of drastic change, it is the learners who inherit the future. The learned usually find themselves equipped to live in a world that no longer exists." (Eric Hoffer)

Richard Bellis

Richard Bellis is an Emmy award-winning composer, author of The Emerging Composer: An Introduction to the People, Problems, and Psychology of the Film Music Business *(Richard Bellis, 2007), and a past president of the Society of Composers & Lyricists. He served on the faculty of the University of Southern California and on the Board of Governors for the Academy of Television Arts and Sciences. He mentors the participants of the ASCAP Television and Film Scoring Workshop with Richard Bellis. He currently serves on the Board of Directors of ASCAP.*

Is the traditional music business dead?

Not dead but in a coma. We'll see what changes there are when the patient wakes up.

Will CDs eventually disappear completely, displaced by digital files?

Yes. Just like vinyl.

Is placing music on sites such as SoundCloud or ReverbNation a viable way for emerging artists to gain visibility and success in the market?

Visibility yes, by other aspiring songwriters and composers. Success? Who knows? It depends on how one defines success. Is merely being well known success? Is being able to support yourself and your family success? Is being a major entertainment "star" success?

Is fan funding a good method for achieving success?

Fans are also consumers. They will react proportionately in the same manner consumers do. Some will support; others will take whatever is offered without feeling any obligation to support.

Will the music-distribution model change from downloading to streaming? Completely or partially?

A combination. There will be things you want to keep and one-time things to satisfy curiosity. I don't believe that consumers will want to subscribe to cloud storage just to keep terabytes of media when it is all available on any device at any time. They certainly will not want to buy large-capacity drives to store their media on.

Do you think the current pricing structure for downloading digital music is a good one? (On average, $1.29 for singles, $9.99 for albums.) How about the pricing models for streaming digital music on sites like Spotify or Rdio? (For example, $0.00029 per stream.)

With or without P2P and piracy? If revenue only flows from 1 out of 10 or 1 out of 100 listeners, the business model for both distributors and creators would have to adjust to reflect those numbers.

What should be done about protecting intellectual property in the digital age? If SOPA (Stop Online Piracy Act) and PIPA (Protect Intellectual Property Act) are not the answer, what is?

God only knows. Literally.

Do you believe that music has been devalued in the last 10 years? If so, can anything be done to change the trend?

In fishing terms, music has become the "bait" rather than the "catch" itself—being offered free on the Internet to lure people to a site that receives revenue from sponsors.

Has getting airplay on Top 40 radio been replaced by licensing music for film or television programs? (Whether it is done directly or through a music library.)

Replaced, no. As an offset to radio's declining numbers, yes.

Do you think that music supervisors are the new A&R people in today's marketplace?

No.

What guidance would you give to the emerging artist who is trying to reach some degree of success in today's music market, whether as a musician, songwriter, or composer?

Consider the healthcare field as an alternative.

Amy Houck

Amy Houck is the CEO and founder of 440 Artist Alignment, a frontier marketing company that specializes in artist development via social media. She comes from a background working as a marketing and design executive with Universal Music Group, Island Def Jam, Geffen, Motown, and many other indie labels. Her expertise lies in the areas of design, development, and branding.

In 2007, Amy moved to LA and was hired at Universal Music Group. She was part of NetReach, the first online marketing department of its kind and a frontier company in social media development for music artists.

Amy marketed and branded a vast variety of clients, such as the Dream, Mariah Carey, Rihanna, Duffy, Queen, LL Cool J, the Killers, the Lonely Island, Ludo, Ne-Yo, Kanye West, Common, LMFAO, Rascal Flatts, Taylor Swift, and many more. She was also one of the designers responsible for branding and designing the Universal Music Group YouTube Channel, which was the first channel on all of YouTube to get one billion views and one million subscribers.

In 2009, she resigned and formed her own successful artist promotion company, 440 Artist Alignment, and in 2011, she wrote her first book, Social Media Secrets for Musicians *(Amy Houck, 2011), a top seller on Amazon. She is extending her reach in 2012 with the formation of Ion Music Group, a California-based record label that specializes in artist development via social media.*

Do you think it is possible to be successful in the "new" music business without relying on a label? (*Success* being defined as "making a living," not necessarily becoming a superstar.)

Yes, it is absolutely possible to be successful in this business without a label. I have been working with successful artists the last five years, and 90 percent do not have a label. Some are young and upcoming musicians that wanted to make a social media splash on their own; others are older musicians with long successful careers in this business and decided against a label for their new project. The key thing both types of musicians need to remember is that being successful takes dedication and time. You have to have a realistic budget that you need to spend, and not just money—*time* is equally important. To have a successful career, you need to have a successful plan, and you need to plan on doing a marketing campaign, whether you hire a company or are doing it yourself. There are tons of ways to *learn* how to promote your music: blogs, Facebook, Twitter, YouTube. The very best advice I can ever give to a musician doing it on their own is, *keep doing it*—go to showcases, play out, and don't push your content down people's throats on Facebook. Find creative ways to make posts—use a quote, say some silly statistic first, use a crazy picture. *No one* wants to see a chat box pop up that says, "Listen to xxxxx link."

Is the traditional music business dead?

We are in a beautiful age of technology and social media. We can reach people in seconds; Twitter "is faster than earthquakes," literally. With that being said, I would say technology rebirthed the traditional music business. Some traditional elements remain, but overall it is very different. Think of it like a child that slightly resembles its parent; they look alike in some respects, but they are very different. In the traditional sense, if the stars aligned you were offered a record deal, but if you didn't sell enough units, you were pushed to the bottom of the barrel. And if you *did* sell enough, then you were off on the path of touring, radio, etc, living fairly well with the weak percentage of money you were making in comparison to the labels. I have a huge issue with the amount of money traditional labels made in comparison with the artists. You would not believe how many dinners I have had with *huge* artists who are now making less than a mechanic. Today, though, there is so much ease with creating your content and placing it on iTunes, YouTube, etc. Two words for upcoming artists: *artist development*. You need it. Rome wasn't built in a day, but then again, Rome endorsed the idea of killing as a sport, so I'm not sure I'd really trust them. (Labels can be Rome.) The point is, it takes time to build something amazing. If your music is meant for the world, the world will hear it; you are not given a gift on accident.

Will CDs eventually disappear completely, displaced by digital files?

There is still space for old records, and vintage will continue to entice generation after generation. But overall in a commercial society, yes.

Is placing music on sites such as SoundCloud or ReverbNation a viable way for emerging artists to gain visibility and success in the market?

SoundCloud is great; Mashable just announced they hit 10 million users. Here is what I have to say about Reverb: When was the last time *you* went to Reverb to discover some cool new music? Get my point? It's too pushy. No one uses it to *find* new material, just musicians to *push* theirs. An alternative: Put your music on Spotify or Pandora.

Is fan funding a good method for achieving success?

Yes! In 2011, our artists total raised just shy of $240,000. It works; it's amazing. Kickstarter is great! It doesn't matter if you live in Bumbletown or a big city, you can do this. The thing is, a lot more people support their friends and musicians than I think they realize.

Will the music distribution model change from downloading to streaming? Completely or partially?

I'm not sure about this yet. Every month I keep comparing sales reports of streaming revenue versus downloading. I need more data to be able to sway one way or the other on this.

Do you think the current pricing structure for downloading digital music is a good one? (On average, $1.29 for singles, $9.99 for albums.) How about the pricing models for streaming digital music on sites like Spotify or Rdio? (For example, $0.00029 per stream.)

The pricing model isn't terrible. The issue is still with how much the artist is making with whoever is hosting the service. I have only one issue with TuneCore; you cannot price your *own* album. Five-dollar albums would be a great idea. If they want to try it, they should test it as a "$5 Album October" and let artists promote this for them.

What should be done about protecting intellectual property in the digital age? If SOPA (Stop Online Piracy Act) and PIPA (Protect Intellectual Property Act) are not the answer, what is?

SOPA—OMG, don't get me started. They way some people talk about this it is almost like they never looked at online media. I hate to see the social media baby in a grown man's body discussing what he doesn't understand yet.

Do you believe that music has been devalued in the last 10 years? If so, can anything be done to change the trend?

The recording process has been devalued; people just record anything and put it out there. It is destroying the ears of our children. There is literally a test you can do with MP3s to see what is missing from the raw WAV, and it's shocking.

Has getting airplay on Top 40 radio been replaced by licensing music for film or television programs? (Whether it is done directly or through a music library.)

Airplay is still important. Licensing and TV can really break an artist, though—"Jar of Hearts." But then again getting your music heard in this world can be a very trying experience.

Do you think that music supervisors are the new A&R people in today's marketplace?

Not at all. They are amazing, talented people. But they are no A&R's—they can sense what is perfect for a mood, a scene, a style. But to be able to predict and assist in an artist's future, that is not what they do.

What guidance would you give to the emerging artist who is trying to reach some degree of success in today's music market, whether as a musician, songwriter, or composer?

The Internet has an answer to just about any question you can ask. Before you ask an expert, do a little research; they will respect you more, and you will have a conversation that leads you to the next step. You have to always be doing things that get you to the next step. And don't believe the hype; the industry is run on talent, and at the end of each day, that's you. *You know it. They know it.* Don't *ever* accept less then what you deserve. *Ever.*

Lastly, is there anything else you'd like to add?

Something you can do right now to take a step forward: Go to Google and find an artist who is similar to you and who is having a successful career, and find out what magazines and blogs are featuring them, and where they are playing out, and piggyback their whole campaign. The same 23-year-old blogger who *loved* their music, odds are, is going to love yours if you are really that similar. And never again post YouTube links *without* clever comments in a chat box on Facebook; this type of activity should be illegal. LOL!

Sarah Gavigan

Sarah Gavigan is a music supervisor and founder/author of the groundbreaking online educational resource Get Your Music Licensed. *With more than a decade of experience as an award-winning music supervisor, Gavigan has created a unique online community as the platform to share her insight and expertise on the notoriously hard to access music licensing industry.*

"After years of being asked the same question, 'How do I get my music licensed?' I decided I was ready to give teaching a try. Soon after, UCLA graciously allowed me to develop and teach my own course in the summer of 2009 and again in the winter of 2010. The natural next step was to write a book, but when I began to see the trend of online learning and the incredible benefits for both the writer and the reader/student, I changed course and developed my entire platform online."

Gavigan has spent the majority of her professional life as an entrepreneur, almost by accident. After owning and running her own talent agency for seven years, Gavigan was drawn to the burgeoning world of music licensing by a conversation started in a van in Iceland in 1999. The conversation with Eric Hilton of Thievery Corporation led Gavigan to understand that indies were interested in finding a way to get their music to brands and agencies. In 2000, Ten Music was born to provide exactly that service to the growing indie music community.

Gavigan pioneered a business model that enabled representation for Indies, allowing their music access to the brightest and best in the vast national advertising network. Gavigan began to dedicate 100 percent of her time to establishing and building a divergent new business model of music representation and branding.

Pairing her passion for independent music with her innate entrepreneurial spirit, Gavigan knew she'd found a distinct niche. Her outspoken thought leadership has defined Gavigan as an industry expert.

Today, Gavigan is a music supervisor/producer for advertising agencies worldwide, consulting for brands on music licensing and writing about her experiences in music licensing and the music industry. Gavigan has presented at workshops and conferences around the globe, including CMJ, SXSW, and Belfast Music Week.

She, her husband Brad, and her beautiful daughter Augusta reside in Nashville. When she's not hunting for new music or checking out a live music show, Sarah can be found cooking in her outdoor woodfire oven.

Do you think it is possible to be successful in the "new" music business without relying on a label? (*Success* being defined as "making a living," not necessarily becoming a superstar.)

Absolutely. You have to choose a great team first and foremost. If that team turns out to be a label, then so be it, but it is not the only option these days. Look at Grammy-winning band the Civil Wars. They have built a completely independent career in less than two years, and they won a Grammy. It's more than possible, it's happening.

Is the traditional music business dead?

As defined in the Long Tail, the major labels and publishers controlled the distribution channels, so the only way to release a record was through them, but no longer. You can do it any way you like! The model from the '90s and before is gone. You simply cannot do what you did then and survive. The majors have been slower to adopt new methods and have certainly not pushed the boundaries the way one might have hoped, but it only opens up more room for other players.

Is placing music on sites such as SoundCloud or ReverbNation a viable way for emerging artists to gain visibility and success in the market?

I think an artist has to use *all* viable social networking options. Why wouldn't you? Most of these services are free; the only thing it costs you is time.

Do you think the current pricing structure for downloading digital music is a good one? (On average, $1.29 for singles, $9.99 for albums.) How about the pricing models for streaming digital music on sites like Spotify or Rdio? (For example, $0.00029 per stream.)

I am more concerned with public performance and digital royalty rates. To date, the three performing rights groups have not been able to reorganize the royalty system to function in today's world. As a writer, there is no way to tell *how* you are making money, no way to estimate and no way to audit. As downloading decreases and streaming increases, this is going to become increasingly important as a revenue stream to artists. Musicians and music professionals need to get educated and involved in bringing light to this issue.

Do you believe that music has been devalued in the last 10 years? If so, can anything be done to change the trend?

Sadly, yes, it has…but we have to consider that the era of the Long Tail is well upon us. In a time when less music was made and distributed, its value was higher. Today, a musician can release his or her own record on iTunes. More music equals less value. It's supply and demand.

Has getting airplay on Top 40 radio been replaced by licensing music for film or television programs? (Whether it is done directly or through a music library.)

There are two factors at play when you consider that music placement can be as powerful as radio. One, distribution. A placement in a major ad campaign can put your music into the ears of millions of people in an instant, and now that most brands also post their commercials on YouTube, the ripple effect is real and longer lasting. Look at the band Fun, who licensed their song "We Are Young" to the Chevy Sonic Super Bowl ad. Less than a week after the commercial aired, it was playing on the radio. In this case, not only did a placement replace the strategy of radio to break a band, but it predicated it! Two, repetition. The second reason that licensing your music to an ad or TV show can compete with the power of radio is repetition. The first time you hear a song, you might not like it, but the hundredth time, you probably do.

Do you think that music supervisors are the new A&R people in today's marketplace?

Without a doubt, but even though I hold this title, it worries me a little. A&R choose music that they think people will enjoy. The main criteria. Music supervisors choose music that is licensable. If a track is licensable, it does not mean that it's good, and vice versa.

What guidance would you give to the emerging artist who is trying to reach some degree of success in today's music market, whether as a musician, songwriter, or composer?

Educate yourself. Don't wait to be discovered; invest in your own career, and you will find that either you enjoy the control and creativity it takes to run your own career, or you will know a heck of a lot more when someone is representing you and will be able to make educated decisions for yourself.

Salme Dahlstrom

Swedish-born singer Salme Dahlstrom stormed onto the electronic music scene in 2008 with her critically acclaimed album The Acid Cowgirl Audio Trade, *featuring the super-catchy "C'mon Y'All," a song that has been featured in ad campaigns for everything from Kellogg's to Juicy Couture to Mitsubishi.* The Wall Street Journal *crowned her "The Licensing Queen" after all of the songs from Salme's album got licensed, a first-time feat for a female artist.*

A DIY indie artist, Salme writes and produces all her own material, in addition to playing most instruments herself. She runs her own record label, Kontainer Music.

Born in the countryside of Sweden, Salme began studying classical music at the age of four. She spent her teenage years writing songs and performing with local bands. She traveled to the U.S. in 1999, where she soon sparked a buzz in the music scene leading the NYC underground band aboyandagirl. With Salme center stage, an aboyandagirl show delivered live music with a passion and energy that matched the best. Within a year of its creation, aboyandagirl were signed to RuffLife/Warner Records. Salme went solo in 2003. She currently resides in New York City.

Do you think it is possible to be successful in the "new" music business without relying on a label? (*Success* being defined as "making a living," not necessarily becoming a superstar.)

I know it is possible because I am doing it. I started my own record label, Kontainer Music—that's where I put out my albums. From a major label point of view, my record sales have been modest, but I have been very successful in licensing my music for use in commercials, movies, and TV. The income from licensing allows me a decent budget for promotion for my releases, as well as pays me a generous salary.

Is the traditional music business dead?

I don't think it's dead, but it is definitely wounded. There are still some great artists coming up the traditional way (Estelle, Lady Gaga), but I think there could be a lot more if the major labels supported their artists beyond the first single, put great albums together rather than just one great song, and signed more real artists instead of reality stars, models, and actors. Just my two cents...

Are placements with music libraries supplanting traditional avenues for composers and songwriters to break into the business?

It's definitely a new way to break into the business. If you do it well, you're bound to get noticed, and that could lead to other gigs, a publishing deal, record deal, who knows.

How does a songwriter or composer begin the process of licensing their music as another means of generating income?

First make sure you control both the publishing and the master rights to your songs (and before that, make sure you write great songs). Sign songwriter and master split agreements with all co-writers/master owners, giving you the right to license your songs and establish how you will split the monies coming in. If you don't have full control over your tracks, you will run into problems both with the licensing companies and with your co-writers.

Submit your music to the reputable music-licensing companies. All companies have their own process for how to submit material, so check out their websites and do as they tell you.

When sending MP3s, always fill in all the info (song title, artist, writers, cover art, etc.) so that when the licensing agent or music supervisor pops your songs into their iTunes, all the info is right there.

Instrumental mixes are as important as your vocal mixes. Always submit instrumentals with your songs submissions.

Will CDs eventually disappear completely, displaced by digital files?

I hope not, but it sure looks like it's already happening. I read an article the other day that said the major labels have decided to only release CDs for major artists' albums and special releases starting in 2012. If that's the case, we're almost there. Another step in that direction is that iTunes has started a "mastered for iTunes" section to better the sound of the digital files, and they're trying to up the bit rate to 24 bit. I'd hate to see CDs go, just like I hated seeing the vinyl disappear. I love the feeling of holding an album, checking out the artwork, reading the lyrics. If CDs disappeared, that would go, too. Digital booklets just don't do it for me.

Is placing music on sites such as SoundCloud or ReverbNation a viable way for emerging artists to gain visibility and success in the market?

I think it's good to be all over the Internet, on credible sites where music fans come to discover new music. But I also think it's very important to have your own official website and to have all your postings on other websites link to your website as much as possible. The longer someone roams your cool, unique-looking site, the more likely they are to sign up for your mailing list and buy a CD—something that you can't set up on many of the other sites. (People can "like" you on Facebook, but that doesn't give you their email address, a very valuable tool in marketing these days.) And you can spend months adding friends on MySpace just to discover that everyone ditched them for Facebook and you're back to square one. Your own website may cost a little to set up, but I think it's money well spent.

Is fan funding a good method for achieving success?

It's good if you have no money and your fans are willing to give to you. I don't know how often that really works, though.

Will the music-distribution model change from downloading to streaming? Completely or partially?

I don't know; I think it's too early to tell. Personally, I prefer downloading music to streaming it, at least when I know the song, but I don't see a reason why both can't coexist. Streaming can be a great tool for discovering new music.

Do you think the current pricing structure for downloading digital music is a good one? (On average, $1.29 for singles, $9.99 for albums.) How about the pricing models for streaming digital music on sites like Spotify or Rdio? (For example, $0.00029 per stream.)

Yes.

What should be done about protecting intellectual property in the digital age? If SOPA (Stop Online Piracy Act) and PIPA (Protect Intellectual Property Act) are not the answer, what is?

Something like SOPA and PIPA is needed, but whatever the act, it needs to take into account all parties involved (like for instance the indie artist), something SOPA and PIPA in my mind did not do.

Do you believe that music has been devalued in the last 10 years? If so, can anything be done to change the trend?

It has, yes. I think a lot more people nowadays think that music should be free or at least much cheaper than in the past. These are the same people who gladly pay $50 for a video game. I have no idea what to do to change the trend; I really wish I did.

Has getting airplay on Top 40 radio been replaced by licensing music for film or television programs? (Whether it is done directly or through a music library.)

I don't think it has replaced radio—getting played on Top 40 radio is still tremendous PR, but getting your music prominently placed on a hit TV show or a commercial can do wonders for your sales as well.

Do you think that music supervisors are the new A&R people in today's marketplace?

For sure. I have found music supervisors to be very open to new sounds and artists. They keep their ear to the ground and have given some amazing new artists great exposure.

What guidance would you give to the emerging artist who is trying to reach some degree of success in today's music market, whether as a musician, songwriter, or composer?

Write the best songs you can, perform with your heart on your sleeve, and be prepared for a ton of rejection. Don't care about trends, do what you love. And only get into it if you really want this. It's hard work, but the rewards can be amazing.

Lastly, is there anything else you'd like to add?

I feel so blessed to be able to make music for a living. I've had a quite unorthodox career, but it's still going and I couldn't be happier. Well, if you all could go out and buy my new CD, actually that would make me even happier. Never give up on your dreams....

Sara Griggs

Sara Griggs Media is a fully integrated Los Angeles–based PR firm specializing in pro audio, music technology brands, and partnerships in artist relations. SGM combines traditional PR practices with utilizing the cutting-edge developments of digital and social media. Launched in 2002, the Sara Griggs Media name has acquired a foundation of service, a reputation of personalized campaigns, and solid relationships with the press.

SGM recently brought their experiences to mobile brands and emerging artist development. Playing a key role in launching clients into new divisions in the mobile sector, SGM highlights the transformation of traditional products into on-the-go mobile applications complete with the same innovative capabilities as the original models. SGM has been honored to lead campaigns including Tascam's Portastudio, Propellerhead's ReBirth, and Line 6's Mobile In and Mobile Keys. The growing artist division, Green Room Artist Relations, is a select roster of independent artists supported by SGM's stable of music-industry professionals and taste-making media.

Sara Griggs started her music career at Mercury Records, where she learned the ropes working on CD launches and tour support for a large roster of artists that included Vanessa Williams, Michelle Shocked, Robert Cray, Bon Jovi, James, Tears for Fears, Texas, and Catherine Wheel. She went on to Roland Corp as a PR and artist relations specialist and was marketing manager at Music Player Network (Guitar Player, Bass Player, EQ, and Keyboard).

SGM clients have included AMS Neve, Beatport, Cerwin Vega, Digidesign, KRK Speakers, Line 6, Mixed In Key, Sasha Soundlab, Stanton DJ, Tascam, and Propellerhead Software—creators of the renowned software Reason.

Sara launched Sara Griggs Media in July 2002 (www.saragriggsmedia.com).

Do you think it is possible to be successful in the "new" music business without relying on a label? (*Success* being defined as "making a living," not necessarily becoming a superstar.)

The "new" music business has enabled musicians to participate in the music industry in ways that just were not possible 10 years ago. Technology has democratized the music industry, but to actually make a living you still first and foremost have to have big talent and tenacity. The musicians that I see making a living are also the ones who have mastered creating and recording with all of the available software. They ultimately have more control over their product and have lower operating costs.

One of my clients, the founder of Propellerhead Software, Ernst Nathorst-Böös, wrote this for a panel that Propellerhead presented at Belfast Music Week:

"Being a musician today means composing, writing, playing, singing, arranging, recording, producing, mixing, mastering, videoing, uploading, designing, promoting, booking, performing, blogging, messaging, and filing tax returns. And all you wanted was some sex!"

Is the traditional music business dead?

The traditional music business is dead for indie artists. It's not dead for superstars.

Will CDs eventually disappear completely, displaced by digital files?

CDs will definitely disappear completely.

Is placing music on sites such as SoundCloud or ReverbNation a viable way for emerging artists to gain visibility and success in the market?

SoundCloud is a great service for artists and such an easy way to get their music out into the world. A great example of how technology is serving the unknown artist.

Is fan funding a good method for achieving success?

Fan funding can be really successful for many artists. The main problem that I have come across is that a lot of artists don't feel comfortable asking for money and support. It's a hustle that takes a certain type of personality, and maybe it's one that isn't always congruous with an artistic personality. It's not as easy as simply having the marketing tools available to them—this is where tenacity becomes vital. But of course, there's a fine line between tenacity and aggression, and artists have to learn where that line is.

Will the music-distribution model change from downloading to streaming? Completely or partially?

I believe that it will move to streaming completely. I also think consumers will not own the music they purchase anymore. It won't be unlimited usage for a one-time fee.

Do you think the current pricing structure for downloading digital music is a good one? (On average, $1.29 for singles, $9.99 for albums.) How about the pricing models for streaming digital music on sites like Spotify or Rdio? (For example, $0.00029 per stream.)

I think eventually consumers will be charged the way broadcasters are charged today. Consumers will pay based on their usage, perhaps monitored and paid for directly from their devices.

What should be done about protecting intellectual property in the digital age? If SOPA (Stop Online Piracy Act) and PIPA (Protect Intellectual Property Act) are not the answer, what is?

This is such a problem. Since I work with leading software companies, like Propellerhead Software, I know firsthand how frustrating this is for the brilliant people who spend a lot of time and money developing incredible products, and for the musicians, their music. Suing 12-year-olds was a PR disaster for the record labels. Ultimately, it comes down to communicating nonstop to consumers. I personally don't see how this problem will be solved.

Do you believe that music has been devalued in the last 10 years? If so, can anything be done to change the trend?

I think it has been devalued, but only to get the consumer hooked on the new way of experiencing music. When iTunes launched, spending 99 cents on a song was so cool!

As I mentioned, I believe that music is going to get a lot more expensive over the next 10 years.

Has getting airplay on Top 40 radio been replaced by licensing music for film or television programs? (Whether it is done directly or through a music library.)

Absolutely. The artists that we represent at Green Room Artist Relations all want film and TV placements. That is an area that they have been successful in and are making some money. Top 40 radio seems an even harder goal to accomplish than it did 10 years ago.

Do you think that music supervisors are the new A&R people in today's marketplace?

The really good ones are.

What guidance would you give to the emerging artist who is trying to reach some degree of success in today's music market, whether as a musician, songwriter, or composer?

Be professional. As simple as that sounds, I can't tell you how many artists approach us that don't have a basic understanding about how to conduct themselves in a business situation.

Choose some industry people that you admire and reach out (in a professional manner, of course!) to them. Yes, you'll be rejected and ignored, but you'll also be surprised at who actually might take the time to help you. Do your homework on the person/company and know in advance what your goals are.

Be consistent. If you let weeks or months lapse without blogging or writing new music or performing or reaching out to grow your fan base, you lose momentum.

Be authentic. When utilizing social media, do it yourself. Don't let your manager, mom, girlfriend/boyfriend do it for you. Communicate with your fans in your authentic voice. If you don't know what to say, find your voice! Also, aside from authenticity, my other important social media advice is don't just ask for things—nobody likes a taker. Try to also be a giver.

Be grateful. A simple thank you goes a long way.

Lastly, is there anything else you'd like to add?

Lastly, talent trumps everything, so hone your craft every single day.

Fawn

Fawn is an award-winning ASCAP singer, songwriter, composer, and recording artist who has shared the top of the Billboard Dance Charts with Lady Gaga, Mariah Carey, and Janet Jackson with her song "Wish U Love," which went to number 6. Her songs can be heard in film and TV shows such as The Natalee Holloway Story, The Young and the Restless, Ugly Betty, Charlie's Angels, Supernatural, *and* CSI Miami.

Fawn was the 2011 Cover Model of the Year for LargeInCharge *magazine and appears in the 2012 coffee-table book* A Day in My Shoes: Pumps and Pups. *www.fawnmusic.com. On IMDB: Fawn II.*

Do you think it is possible to be successful in the "new" music business without relying on a label? (*Success* being defined as "making a living," not necessarily becoming a superstar.)

Yes. I think that *anything* is possible!

Is the traditional music business dead?

In many ways it has died, and in many ways it has not. There are only a couple of big labels left. Live performance and TV and film licensing are bigger than ever. Sadly, it has stayed the same as far as taking advantage of the artist, and in some cases, basically raping them.

Will CDs eventually disappear completely, displaced by digital files?

I hope not. I think that they will not necessarily disappear, but become as vinyl records have—a thing of the past, with a resurgence of popularity. I recently ordered a turntable that plugs into my computer so I can transfer all of my vinyls into iTunes. Although I will never throw away my vinyls, it is much more convenient to have them in my iPhone and iPod for the car and for on the go. I think that we are a "fast food" society—speedy consumption and quick convenience. This need is what will drive us to all digital, which I think will be our demise in the end.

Is placing music on sites such as SoundCloud or ReverbNation a viable way for emerging artists to gain visibility and success in the market?

Yes. I think that virtually *any* online publicity is a productive tool for an artist or entertainer. I was on the site MusicFreedom, which was created by music veterans and backed by JC Chasez. The site has been defunct for a few years now, but during the time I was on there (four years out of the four-and-a-half years that they were up and running), I was the number-one electronic artist, as well as the number-five and number-four artist of *all* genres there. It not only motivated me to keep going, I found some incredible talent (and horrible talent) on there, established relationships, and made connections, which spilled over to my MySpace pages and have now continued over to my three Facebook pages.

Is fan funding a good method for achieving success?

I have yet to do that, but some people have had great success doing it. I know that the band Marillion reportedly raised $725,000 by pre-selling its *Anoraknophobia* double-CD album before it was even recorded, and when I had spoken to Jill Sobule, she had raised over $80,000 from 500 fans to record her 2009 album, *California Years*. So, the answer is *yes*. There are veteran artists on the ArtistShare website, such as Siedah Garrett and actor Rick Moranis. I think we have been forced into fan funding because of all the piracy on the Internet.

Will the music-distribution model change from downloading to streaming? Completely or partially?

No, because people are always going to want to have physical copies that they can move around.

Do you think the current pricing structure for downloading digital music is a good one? (On average, $1.29 for singles, $9.99 for albums.) How about the pricing models for streaming digital music on sites like Spotify or Rdio? (For example, $0.00029 per stream.)

I think for now it's fair. It seems to be working. This pricing structure basically saved the music industry from going into oblivion when iTunes came out. When iTunes first came out, no one believed it would work; everyone was skeptical, but it did! It opened the door for independent artists and saved the seasoned artists.

What should be done about protecting intellectual property in the digital age?

We need some kind of copy protection that won't limit the consumer, but will slow down or (in a perfect world) stop the pirates on the Internet. One thing that may help is changing audio files to high def, which will have a new copy protection scheme built in, but will add much more value to the digital file. For example, if you could download Pink Floyd's *The Wall* in 5.1 surround, that would give added value to the consumer, which would make it worth their while to buy. However, I think someone will always be able to find a way to copy something, unfortunately.

If SOPA (Stop Online Piracy Act) and PIPA (Protect Intellectual Property Act) are not the answer, what is?

We need to come up with a scaled system of enforcement. If we punish the person that steals a pack of gum with the same sentence as someone who robs a bank, it isn't fair and won't pass. I'd like to see a list of names of the people who have downloaded for free, and then have them charged for the money they've stolen. And if they don't pay, it goes on their credit report and criminal record, depending on the volume of theft.

Do you believe that music has been devalued in the last 10 years? If so, can anything be done to change the trend?

Yes, I believe that music has become devalued in the past 10 years. What's ironic is its importance to our souls has *not* gone down in value. We are living in an age where kids and young adults think that a song is worth only $1.29 or 99 cents—or worse yet, *free*. When in reality, a song is *priceless*. Songwriters are having their intellectual property continually stolen, because once a song hits iTunes or even

YouTube, it can be downloaded for free. My hit song "Wish U Love," which was number-six on the Billboard Dance charts in 2010, was downloaded more than 20,000 times on free download sites in its first six months. If I had had even 50 cents for each of those, I would have made my money back on the song and been able to record the next single release. ASCAP has been policing as much as they can, but music is still falling in between the cracks of the Internet, and artists are unable to continue to create and live their dream because of this. It's very sad.

Has getting airplay on Top 40 radio been replaced by licensing music for film or television programs? (Whether it is done directly or through a music library.)

No. It seems that the real promotion happening for music these days *is* through shows such as *American Idol*, *The Voice*, and *America's Got Talent*. But the radio will always be important, I think. Look at how well Sirius is doing.

Do you think that music supervisors are the new A&R people in today's marketplace?

No. I think that the new A&R person is the artist him/herself. It's up to them to fly their own "freak flag high."

What guidance would you give to the emerging artist who is trying to reach some degree of success in today's music market, whether as a musician, songwriter, or composer?

Network, network, network! Trademark yourself in your style and your look. Be positive. No one likes a negative drain. The industry is hard enough; we don't need more negativity around. People don't like to work with stuck-up divas or difficult people. This business is big but very small, and word will get around quickly. Put yourself out on every social network, socialize with your "fans," be part of their lives, be honest and humble. Work on your craft; record record-ready/radio-ready material, not demos; and come up with a six-month plan. Re-evaluate your plan every few months. If you have a clear goal in your mind, you will make it. Do live shows, tour, create merchandise, don't be afraid to work for free at times, and have a business card with your photo on it so people remember who you are when they see you.

Lastly, is there anything else you'd like to add?

Don't compromise your morals to get ahead. Because in the end, you will be going backwards if you do.

Kelli Richards

Kelli Richards is an industry icon and visionary in the convergence of Silicon Valley, Hollywood, and Madison Avenue, with deep expertise in digital distribution, branded content, and social engagement. She is a pioneer in creating the earliest "direct-to-fan" strategies for established artists. Kelli served at Apple for 10 years, driving music initiatives, and helped to birth a whole new movement for artists and fans alike as a thought-leader in digital music.

Kelli has served as an advisor to disruptive, innovative companies and established artists alike—and as a trusted, sought-after, high-level strategic consultant, coach, and executive for more than 15 years. She is the author of two bestselling books on digital music and social media in music.

As a highly sought-after consultant, mentor, speaker, producer, coach, and author, Kelli is the CEO of the All Access Group. She and her team facilitate strategic business opportunities in digital distribution between technology companies, established artists and celebrities, film studios, record labels, and consumer brand companies in order to foster new revenue streams and deliver compelling consumer experiences.

Kelli has sat on the San Francisco chapter of the Board of Governors for the National Academy of Recording Arts and Sciences (NARAS), which is the producer of the Grammy Awards. She holds a BS in Business Administration and an MBA, both from San Jose State University.

She has co-authored two books, including the critically acclaimed The Art of Digital Music: 56 Artists, Visionaries & Insiders Reveal Their Creative Secrets *(Backbeat Books, 2004). She is also a Certified Integrative Life Coach trained under best-selling authors and coaches Debbie Ford and Alan Cohen. She lives in Cupertino, California, in the heart of the Silicon Valley.*

Do you think it is possible to be successful in the "new" music business without relying on a label? (*Success* being defined as "making a living," not necessarily becoming a superstar.)

Absolutely! This was the premise that Todd Rundgren and I had when we launched the earliest "artist 360, direct-to-fan" venture called PatroNet in the mid-'90s. When you as an artist retain 80 to 90 percent of your revenues from all sources and build a good-sized following of, say, at least 50,000 dedicated fans (or so), you can make a decent living as a musician without the need for a bunch of other middlemen who would otherwise take large chunks of your revenues, leaving you with little.

Is the traditional music business dead?

I wouldn't say it's dead so much as the underpinnings of how the business work have morphed and changed dramatically over the past decade. The artist is now in the power position versus the label, and things aren't done in a linear fashion anymore. The music business worked essentially the same way for more than 50 years, and in the past decade of disruption and disintermediation, there are now many more ways an artist can reach his/her fans and make money.

Will CDs eventually disappear completely, displaced by digital files?

I would have said so if you asked me this a decade ago, but it's clear that they haven't. There's a whole generation who would still prefer to buy and own the physical CDs versus buying music digitally (with the fear that the music could go *poof*).

It's taken a lot longer for the displacement and shifts to occur than I would have imagined back then, but we're starting to see digital music sales rising to a great extent and the sale of physical CDs continue to decline; that continues year after year.

How does a songwriter or composer begin the process of licensing their music as another means of generating income?

There are several things they can do. Have an agent who places their music with publishers and/or music supervisors and/or ad agencies. Network and reach out to music supervisors and creative directors at ad agencies directly on their own. (Linked In makes this possible.) As much as possible, attend conferences and events where these folks are speaking. And use services where music supervisors go online to find new music that's not as expensive to license as well-known songs by big artists—for example, www.musicsupervisor.com, www.musicdealers.com, www.reverbnation.com, www.rumblefish.com, and others.

Is placing music on sites such as SoundCloud or ReverbNation a viable way for emerging artists to gain visibility and success in the market?

YES! These and others, like Sonicbids, CD Baby, IODA, and Topspin (among many others) are a must in today's music market in terms of having a presence and making sure you're leveraging the services they offer artists to extend their reach.

Is fan funding a good method for achieving success?

It can be; this was certainly the premise behind the PatroNet service that Todd Rundgren and I founded all those years ago—where artists were essentially underwritten by their fan bases. It's a *great* way to come up with production costs to do your next album *if* you've done a good job in amassing a strong and loyal fan base—and give those "investors" some kind of premium goodies or experiences in exchange (i.e., the chance to buy first and best seats when you tour, the ability to do meet-and-greets with the band at shows, and possibly attend sound checks, the chance to be the first listen to new tracks and the ability to provide feedback, bundle subscriptions to an artist's fan club, and the chance to be the first to receive the finished CDs—these are just some ideas).

Will the music distribution model change from downloading to streaming? Completely or partially?

I think they'll live side by side, so there will be options for the artist and the fans to leverage both as they make sense for different purposes. I don't think streaming will replace downloading per se.

Do you think the current pricing structure for downloading digital music is a good one? (On average, $1.29 for singles, $9.99 for albums.) How about the pricing models for streaming digital music on sites like Spotify or Rdio? (For example, $0.00029 per stream.)

Yes, I do—however, it's an even better model when artists receive more of the proceeds from sale of downloads versus what they would get under a typical recording model in splits with the label; so when that's more at parity it can be quite a lucrative model for an artist with a strong fan following. I think over time the streaming pricing models will get better, too.

What should be done about protecting intellectual property in the digital age? If SOPA (Stop Online Piracy Act) and PIPA (Protect Intellectual Property Act) are not the answer, what is?

This is a controversial topic, and my answer may not be very popular, but I think artists (especially rising artists who are building an audience base) need to let go of making money from their songs—and instead make their money from touring, song placements, merchandise sales, bundles, and all the other ways they can monetize their brand and the artist/fan experience.

Do you believe that music has been devalued in the last 10 years? If so, can anything be done to change the trend?

No, I don't—there have never been more ways for artists to monetize their brands and make good money (make a good living!), especially those who see themselves as a brand and act as such in place-ment and direct-to-fan experiences.

Has getting airplay on Top 40 radio been replaced by licensing music for film or television programs? (Whether it is done directly or through a music library.)

The real question here is whether Top 40 radio is even relevant anymore versus online streaming and satellite radio. Radio in all its formats (terrestrial and other) merely helps to support licensing and all the other spokes on an artist's 360 wheel.

Do you think that music supervisors are the new A&R people in today's marketplace?

Speaking as a former A&R exec myself, I'd say that there are *many* replacements for traditional A&R today; music supervisors certainly are one of the avenues for filtering and curating great new music. But the Internet and social media arenas offer a lot more ways artists can get heard and find their audiences beyond the narrow funnel of traditional A&R.

What guidance would you give to the emerging artist who is trying to reach some degree of success in today's music market, whether as a musician, songwriter, or composer?

The most important thing is to make great music and write good songs; that hasn't ever changed. The second thing is to find and build (cultivate and nurture) your audience—and engage with your fans directly online, via social media, and in person when you're on the road. Those are truly the most important ingredients to success for any artist in today's world.

Lastly, is there anything else you'd like to add?

YES—read all you can from people like myself who are focused on artists. A great new book just came out by a close colleague of mine, Jaunique Sealey, who used to drive social media efforts and digital for Lady Gaga, called *A Piece of the Fame*. My own bestseller, *Taking the Crowd to the Cloud: Social Media in Music*, also offers practical tips for artists. And as importantly, make sure you keep all your rights—to your music, your publishing, and your domain name; find a great team and see yourself as a brand. Be willing to get creative in licensing your music and your brand, and stay connected to your fans!

15 Conclusions, Musings, and Reminders

Is there really any way to come to a conclusion when a story hasn't even reached its third act? I doubt it. But there is always room for speculation, prognostication, and mastication (I like to chew on something while I'm thinking). So I will offer up some of those thoughts for consideration—and how we find ourselves somewhere between Music 1.0 and Music 5.0. That's not to say there won't be a Music 6.0, but we can only chew off a bit at a time, right?

While I was working on this book, which I affectionately referred to as M3 (for *Marketing and Merchandising for Musicians*), I had a realization: You can't have a realistic discussion about marketing and merchandising for musicians without considering the tremendous number of forces at play. These include market conditions, technology, finance, politics, copyright, and other human rights. Does this sound overstated? I don't believe so.

The topics in this final chapter are a combination of gut feelings, facts, deductive reasoning, basic opinion, and unsolicited viewpoints. I'm very happy that I have an opportunity to share some of them.

Market Conditions

The law of supply and demand is about as basic and ancient as you can get. But it still holds water—as well as the key to your present and future status in the music biz. A funny thing happened on the way to the Internet. The freedom of access to content created both a wealth of content and a lowering of its perceived value. It removed the old "filters" of the record industry but replaced them with new filters—even the technology giants (YouTube, Microsoft, Amazon, and so on) pass judgment on what artists get placed front and center and those who do not. The newer kids on the block, from ReverbNation to BandOnABus (I made that one up), look at metrics just as much as the next guy. Who's getting traction? Who's creating buzz? How can we make some money off of this? (That last one was simply transferred from Music 1.0 to Music 2.0 and beyond.)

And speaking of Music 1.0, you may have noticed that some of my observations in various places throughout the book do not put the "old" music business in a favorable spotlight. Without hashing through those arguments again, I will offer yet another viewpoint—and that is that there is still a role, need, and place for the traditional record business, albeit smaller than it once was. Superstars are still being found and launched through the old machine, and older superstars still rely on this machine to get their product distributed in large quantities. I liken it to a typewriter that is obsolete, yet there is still a role for it. True, that role is largely in museums and in a recent resurgence of typewriter worshippers who have just now discovered the device. Nevertheless, never say "never."

Music Glut, the Lottery, and *American Idol*

Although it may sound like it, this is not cynicism. The realities of the music business are as sobering as ever. Further, there's an almost lottery-like aspect to it that didn't exist before, in which someone completely unknown can start selling reasonable amounts of music in a very short time. Ironically, there's a lottery-like aspect to the "regular" music business as well. Take *American Idol*, for example. Take it from "one day you're nobody"—to "the next day you're a superstar." The irony doesn't end there, for beyond the easy access provided by the Internet during difficult market conditions, how many new possible stars would emerge if it weren't for *American Idol*, *The X Factor*, *Prussia's Got Talent*, and the numerous other clones appearing every day?

For any musical need that is broadcast on the web via websites or social sites, there are mountains of responses from qualified and unqualified artists alike. This trend is not bound to reverse itself anytime soon. It is not out of the question that future market forces could alter the equation yet again—but it would have to be in a manner that is almost impossible to imagine at this point. But you're not going to let that discourage you, are you? I know it won't—because you have the fever.

There Is No Twelve-Step for This Malady

Yes, it's a sickness. You have to make music. You can't help it. If you weren't doing this, there's nothing else you could do, right?

Well, that depends on how you look at it. First, there's a semantic issue. If you weren't doing this, there's nothing else you *could* do? Or perhaps what you really mean is there's nothing else you *would* do.

I understand the sentiment completely. Assuming you have some artistic talent, it can be downright impossible to tame the compulsion to create. It can drive you up the wall if you don't have some sort of outlet for it. And in an ideal world, that outlet would give you the income you need to keep creating. It makes perfect sense.

I heard someone of celebrity utter the famous "there's nothing else I could do" line one time. It was at an industry tradeshow, and Hans Zimmer was being interviewed. He used the same words to describe that all-familiar need to create music. The difference, though, is that if you have already achieved the success and stature of a Hans Zimmer, then the idea that there's nothing else you *could* or even *would* do is completely justified. You don't have to worry about it! You've arrived. Pass the champagne and have your people *try* to get a hold of my people!

The difficulty occurs when you're trying to climb that shaky ladder to the top, and now that ladder is missing many of the rungs it once had. The new rungs are still elusive and certainly ever-changing. But in the meantime, you have to support yourself (and likely a few others), and therefore the luxury of refusing to do anything else is a non-starter.

You are a part of the current market conditions that are creating expansion, not contraction or even stability, in this competitive field. Your drive has been further enhanced by the ease with which you can obtain creative tools to realize your musical vision. The old excuses are gone:

"It's only a demo."

"It will sound better in the studio." (You're in your studio, for crying out loud!)

"I couldn't afford to make a quality album." (Then you should quit now.)

"No one believes in me." (You mean a dying record company, or the entire population of Earth?)

You're sick. You have to make music. Don't let anyone stop you. Just make sure you know what is realistic today. Be talented and savvy enough to make a living at it. There used to be gold records, and that was fun. Digital files don't come in gold, but they can be very satisfying nonetheless.

What Will You Be Serving?

What will you serve up for the next stages of the revolution? What drives you? What moves you? What is your definition of success?

The responsibility for the next stages of musical evolution—Music 3.0, 4.0, whatever—have fallen upon you. It may be difficult, but you might be best off extricating yourself from the crowd at large and finding, as is often said in this business, your own voice.

Not moved by money but moved by music.

Not attached to the result but to the process.

Not the guy or gal who lusts after the smash single on radio, but the one who is compelled to say something honest, even at the cost of extreme vulnerability.

Those drivers are what created the music industry of the 1960s, '70s, and '80s in the first place. Perhaps it is time to rewind the revolution.

A Different Look at the Techno Wars

There is probably no chapter in this book that doesn't mention the effects of technology on the music business, whether directly or indirectly. Technology affects every process and facet of the business, including music creation, distribution, licensing, and consumption. Technology changes the rules, and then it changes the rules again. Some remarkable people have made significant changes in more than one of these areas, and of course, Steve Jobs is one who comes to mind.

Those who can bridge the gap between technology and creativity—between the left and the right brain—benefit by possessing a competitive advantage. Those who only understand the technology side not only pose a challenge to us all, but can even present a threat to progress. In general terms, I am concerned about the Googles and Yahoos of the world who—if left to their own devices—would be much happier if the music (like the Internet) was free. Getting technology giants to respect the intellectual property of others has been quite a challenge—and it's mind-boggling to me that while they are super-protective of their own intellectual property, copyrights, and trademarks, they have been very slow to see the connection to other types of content—specifically, music, movies, and books.

So the techno wars—to me, anyway—are becoming less about the ability to advance and deploy technology and more about the ability of technologists to understand and respect the rights of content creators in the creative fields. Although the Googles of the world have made some progress in this regard in recent years, we are all eons away from being able to let down our guard on this topic.

That said, technology does have a way of shaking things up in a huge way. Moore's Law became well known as a rule of thumb for predicting the doubling of chip performance every 18 months. That idea seems almost primitive if you include not just chips, but all facets of technology today. Perhaps we need Moore's Second Law, which states, "Fuhgeddaboudit! Stop thinking about the exponential changes in technology—it'll make your head spin. Just keep creating great products."

Technology, Moore's Law, and the pace of change are unstoppable forces that seem to be mimicking the expansion of the universe itself—everything expanding faster and farther, with no end in sight.

Greed Is Good—or Not

It's as American as apple pie: Every business has a right to make a profit.

Every product or service has a price—and every product or service has a cost. The cost can be the monies required, before profits, for the company to produce the product or service, such as capital equipment, leasehold improvements, or labor. The cost can also be much more than that. It might include the costs in human resources (the emotional kind), morale, life, liberty, and the pursuit of happiness. Yes, indeed, those are all rights guaranteed by the Constitution of the United States of America. But I am not conducting an exercise in patriotism here. I'm merely pointing out that commerce cannot be measured solely in terms of black and white dollars and cents. There are many other things to consider—and as witness, I present the global economic crisis that began in 2007 and continues today.

The Race to the Bottom: No One Wins

What does this have to do with the business of music? Everything. The music business, especially in our Internet age, is a prime example of how costs—beyond the obvious ones—can mount up and affect a whole range of other things: culture, values, progress, and maintaining a core spiritual center that dictates decisions and directions.

Throughout this book I have discussed issues of copyright, piracy, and the "race to the bottom," including the devaluation of music in both perception and price. These issues are admittedly complex and lack a simple, immediate solution. But it is incumbent upon those in the music (and entertainment) business as a whole to deal with them head-on. The adolescent screams of "music should be free" need to be silenced and the screamers educated—unless and until *everything* is free. One group, those who create intellectual property, cannot be singled out as workers—hired hands—who receive no or little remuneration for their work. This is also true on a larger scale, such as the case of Apple vs. Samsung, in which legitimate patents belong to their creators, as validated by the court finding. If a person or company generates a large amount of revenue from their intellectual property, that doesn't mean it's open season for anyone else to come along and borrow (or steal) it.

The responsibility for dealing with and solving these issues rests in the hands of both content creators and, ultimately, legislators. The latter group is, as irony would have it, suffering from the effects of extreme partisanship enhanced by a global economic meltdown. So progress from that group is slow at best—not that it was ever very fast.

The other responsible group—the content creators—is made up of individuals who are silent at worst and ineffectual at best. This group cannot even communicate with and educate the public sufficiently enough so that people understand the intrinsic value of intellectual property. When the proponents of the "music should be free" group complain about the greedy, irresponsible corporate behemoths of the music industry, who surely don't "need" any more profits, the content creators cannot even distinguish themselves from the corporations, who are actually the ones raking in the profit. According to popular perceptions, there is essentially no difference between a record company and a new, emerging songwriter who is struggling to make a living. This is an absurdity. What possible offense is there against someone trying to make a living in a tough business? If you point to a Stevie Wonder or another superstar as an example of a content creator making a good living, you are talking about a tiny, tiny percentage of artists in that category. The rest of us are trying to figure out how to make next month's rent.

Music Industry: Also Guilty as Charged

But there are those in the "new" music business who are just as guilty of playing the greed game. Lawsuits regarding digital royalties are being brought against Sony Music by the Allman Brothers, Cheap Trick, and others. Now Toto (who produced the big hit "Africa") is also suing them because Toto gets 15 percent instead of 50 percent of their rightful royalties. This is because of a new interpretation of digital rights in which some record companies are insisting that digital music is not being "licensed," it is being "leased"—at least, according to Sony.

Spotify is another company that comes to mind. This is a company that pays such small royalties to everyone—record companies, publishers, and by default, artists—that it would take 43 light-years to see any significant monies. Yet, at the same time, Spotify is seeking *billions* in financing to "expand" their business. Do you think they want the money so that they can pay content creators and copyright holders? Really?

So you can probably see that the politics of ownership and copyright easily extend to other rights—human rights and moral rights. You can see that the politics of greed are not restricted to one type of business or even one type of political party. The drivers of fairness in providing royalties to content creators must come from within. If there is no moral basis for doing what's fair, there is little hope for navigating this ship out of troubled waters.

What Does All This Have to Do with M3?

Hopefully, *Marketing and Merchandising for Musicians* contains a lot of practical, everyday strategies for improving your music career in this constantly changing business. In the Internet Age, the responsibility lies largely with you in every aspect of promoting yourself or your band. But your responsibility goes far beyond that. It includes all of the topics I've mentioned from the beginning of this chapter up until now, which are mostly summarized in the previous section, "What Will You Be Serving?"

The subject of ownership rights carries with it issues that are your responsibility to be constantly aware of and to defend, lest you wish to be a penniless musician or simply a casual observer who sees the rights of songwriters and composers collapse into oblivion. Your silence in response to any of these current issues simply grants permission to continue to be violated. Your unwillingness to consider the ramifications that arise when the next guy comes along with the "It's good exposure" argument or "Do it for free just this one time" pronouncement are akin to taking a monetary razorblade to yourself and going to town. These types of decisions require your participation and cannot be produced by anything but your own motivation. The phrase "silence is deafening" could not be any more appropriate for a lack of response when it comes to your music rights.

So if you are going to market yourself and produce merchandise for yourself, there has to be a market, and there has to be a means of creating revenue streams. That's what this book has been about—and I tossed in the insidious, creeping effects of the music/Internet revolution to give it the proper context.

Music revolutions begin well. Rules change. Laws change. You must change with them.

And never forget to go back to your roots—the music itself.

- Honesty cannot be faked in relationships, and when it comes to promoting your music to your fans, your music is the core of that relationship.
- Use all of the tools at your disposal, but always be true to yourself.
- Don't stand idly by while your basic rights are taken from you.
- Know your self-worth—imagine a world without any music, if you can. You can't, can you?

And one final word on the topic of the "old music industry" versus music in the digital age.

We are currently living in a music industry "twilight zone," in which neither the old music industry nor the new digital, social media–driven music business is king.

If you want to disregard the old record business, ask Katy Perry or Lady Gaga if that's a good idea. Each is with a major label—and Katy Perry recently announced the formation of her own label, likely under the Capitol-EMI banner. They wouldn't very likely be enjoying the pop stardom they have now without the engines of these labels driving them.

And if you think the new era of digital, social-media music success is impossible to achieve, just ask Korean pop singer PSY, whose single "Gangham Style" practically took over the world in the summer of 2012. Shared and promoted on YouTube from everyday folks to celebrities including Britney Spears and Tom Cruise, it went to number one on the iTunes charts in more than 30 countries. The song and its artist went on to cause flash mobs and gain media attention in every major print and broadcasting outlet worldwide.

So, it's very hard to accurately predict the future of the music business. But while you're waiting to see which way is up, why not crank out a potential hit or two? You can do it yourself.

Index